3 OF IO

POEMS BY HANK LAZER

CHAX PRESS

TUCSON

1996

Acknowledgements:
I wish to thank the editors of the following magazines and anthologies who have published various portions of *Three of Ten*: *lower limit speech*, *The Art of Practice: 45 Contemporary Poets*, *Salon*, *6ix*, *Poetry USA*, *RIF/T*, *Central Park*, *Temblor*,
Thinker Review, and *Nexus*.
A portion of "Displayspace 7" is included in Dana Wilson's opera "For Stavros" (1991).
Negation was published by Inge Bruggeman's INK-A! Press in an edition of fifty handmade copies, including an audiocassette of the poet reading the entire sequence.
Three of Ten represents three chapters from a longer work-in-progrss, *10 X 10*. The first of these chapters to be published was *INTER(IR)RUPTIONS* (Generator Press, 1992).

Library of Congress Cataloging-in-Publication Data

Lazer, Hank.
3 of 10 : poems / by Hank Lazer.
p. cm.
ISBN 0-925904-18-X (alk. paper)
I. Title. II. Title: Three of ten.
PS3562.A984A615 1996
811'.54—DC20 96-30798
CIP

chax press / box 848 / tucson, arizona 85701-0848

to Linda and Stan Goodman

to my mother, Wendy Lazer

& in memory of my father, Charles Lazer

TABLE OF CONTENTS

H's JOURNAL

for Ron Silliman

who sent us

sentencing

H's JOURNAL

I

May 25, 1990 – June 12, 1990

1 In a show of independence for which no crowing is called for, I went home to spend my fortieth birthday with my parents and my sister, for I have settled deliberately at some distance, knowing that to go home bestirs the confused marrow of one's imagined autonomy.

2 As said in a friend's words: "you do that again, & I'll beat the dog out of you."

3 A distrust of feelings transcendental is itself a bracing tonic.

4 Product of its given day, each sentence a citizen in full.

5 "Like cuttlefish we conceal ourselves, we darken the atmosphere in which we move; we are not transparent."

6 "'Life in the Words' suggests much of the geniuine significance of the book to Thoreau: it was life and self re-created and revised in words, and he lived in the words he had created."

7 Redundant wonder — the learned arpeggio of an appreciative, sensitive observer — amounts to a truncated intellect and failure to recognize the place of rhetoric in governing written (and thus constructed) expression.

8 "He had to hide from himself the pent-up anger of having his ambitions foiled."

9 "Viewed in this light, it is no accident that suicides are so common in the spring."

10 "In human intercourse the tragedy begins not when there is misunderstanding about words, but when silence is not understood."

11 "Let your life be a counter friction to stop the machine."

12 "When you travel to the celestial city, carry no letter of introduction."

13 "Whenever he got too close to success, he was not only exhilarated but scared."

14 Fuchsia Farmers of America.

15 "This strange man, rumor said, had written a book no copy of which had ever been sold."

16 To travel means to become intensely aware, by contrast, of wasted opportunities at home.

17 When on foot for great periods of time, he became acutely subject to the weather, the condition of his knees, and the availability of restrooms.

18 "The fruit a thinker bears is *sentences*."

19 To be a guest is to be both simultaneously in an affable pleasant manner present and to be wished away.

20 Based on what you already know, more than enough self-judgment can be made.

21 By whatever tweezers your rhetorical grasp contaminates the natural object so tweezed, though certain panaromic modes simulate the ego's suspension in a vastly overwhelming solution.

22 Coy turns to arch by twist of comma-laden phrasing.

23 The way certain furniture brings on a sense of helplessness, a child-like dependency all over again, as if you had to ride your bike to get there and no more rapid commanding means availed itself.

24 Ever since my son was born I have not doubted my desire to live.

25 The weight, dear reader, of your expectations is both a blessing and a contemptible form of romantic excess which stems from your ambivalent sense of equality and inferiority.

26 I pace the ornamental widow's walk; I mount, with cause, the lookout; I pray for sight of thee.

27 Certain subjects permit only a tone which conveys, implicitly, that all this is *after* the fact, well after a massively deadly deed to which you have been witness.

28 "In all cases we esteem rather the suggested ideal than the actual man, and it is remarkable that so many men have an actual brother, an improved edition of themselves, to whom we are introduced at last."

29 “In the end, the only escape from these emotions would be death, the ultimate secession from both North and South.”

30 “Thus each wind is self-registering.”

31 “When he had wakeful nights, he would ask me to arrange the furniture so as to make fantastic shadows on the wall, and he wished his bed was in the form of a shell, that he might curl up in it.”

32 “On the ‘beautiful spring morning’ of May 6, 1862, soon after smelling a bouquet of hyacinths and requesting that he be raised in his own bed, his breathing became progressively shallower; at nine o’clock he died peacefully, at the age of forty-four, with his mother, sister, and Aunt Louisa in attendance.”

33 “Channing reported that his last distinct words were ‘moose’ and ‘Indian.’”

34 “This curious world which we inhabit is more wonderful than it is convenient; it is more to be admired and enjoyed than used.”

35 “As the family moved from a producing to a consuming unit, she could have some say in household purchases, such as furnishings and appliances.”

36 “If Henry, whether justifiably or not, held sexual desire responsible for his parents’ marriage (a marriage, he perceived, which had emasculated and entrapped his father, frustrated his mother), then it becomes more understandable why Henry was so distrustful of, and uncomfortable with, his own sexuality.”

37 "Each night I am gathered to my fathers."

38 "I feel myself uncommonly prepared for *some* literary work, but I can select no work."

39 "Almost in proportion to the sincerity and earnestness of the life will be the sadness of the record."

40 "A man can attend but one funeral in the course of his life, can behold but one corpse."

H's JOURNAL

2

June 12, 1990 – June 22, 1990

41 "While others in the vicinity, now aware of the fire, went to town for more help, Thoreau — instead of making efforts to put out the conflagration — set out for the highest rock on Fair Haven Cliff."

42 We play mostly covers but with our own particular twist; we'd like to do more original stuff, but that's not what they want to hear.

43 A proper name, repeated sporadically, provides the illusion of continuity.

44 Of course a journal tells a story, but the story being tracked is indiscernible, involves blurrings, has plenty of string and an equal amount of uncertainty about what are to be its beads.

45 Is the stage definitely already lit and, if so, must you enter and pirouette; and, if so, wearing what?

46 As habitations, some hospitable, some quite extravagant: language, dwelling, being.

47 "How the self comes together with phenomena in the world is always an accident out of which significance is gleaned."

48 He records those thoughts nearest to him which are also the most remote, so that returning to them throughout his remaining years memory and remembering are tinged with strangeness and recovery.

49 "Miller, moreover, chastises Thoreau for being afflicted with a bad case of the transcendentalist's disease in which the more a man loves other men the more passionately he defends the importance of being separate from them."

50 "The man who is dissatisfied with himself — what can he not do?"

51 "Consciousness does not just mediate or mirror natural phenomena; as we see in the following passage, the fiction of the *Journal* is that consciousness is displaced by them."

52 The percentage of humidity, the gray cast, in this case the barrage of semi-vivid abstractions, gives index to the slow passage of summer months.

53 To say more would compromise our relationship.

54 My kinship to Ed Poe consists in our shared imagination of a god who is a master ironist, a jokester, in my case a god given to sentimentality and a love of mediocrity, a god in fact who genuinely loves people who affix bumperstickers which say "God 's you," loves them all the more for the unnecessary apostrophe.

55 If you change your name once, what's to stop you from changing it again and again?

56 "In Perry Miller's facetious and — I think — accurate words: 'Thoreau flouted the highest, the most sacred, duty of masculinity: he was not interested in women.'"

57 Jesus, in spite of compelling parables, won't work as an example of meekness, for in that show he too willingly stars.

58 Meaning comma goes off comma at a tangent comma as the radiant or radial vector comma firing off comma in the pauses provided for comma your own thought processes comma activated by contact comma with this stuff no end stop.

59 As the previously went about a systematic elimination of specific reference to the human, it remained then to accomplish a thorough going erasure of the natural.

60 This town affords one a peculiar opportunity to acquire a literacy of late afternoon thundershowers.

61 It is always with a minor twinge of guilt that I have been drawn into projects (if that term makes any sense in this connection) which cannot be conceived and which in fact of necessity remain endless, incomplete (though sometimes circumscribed).

62 "The 'discipline' of the record depends upon sustaining a project in which the description of natural occurrence cannot, by definition, be 'memorable,' for though these phenomena are to be noted, why they are to be noted evades comprehension."

63 "Do not seek expressions — seek thoughts to be expressed."

64 "After hoeing, or perhaps reading and writing, in the forenoon, I usually bathed again in the pond, swimming across one of its coves for a stint, and washed the dust of labor from my person, or smoothed out the last wrinkle which study had made, and for the afternoon was absolutely free."

65 "And only the most intelligent and stupid can avoid goal-directed work."

66 His method became one of attentive and intensive labor, usually writing, principally of some thought process or extended observation, continued over a period of time until some means of assemblage seemed worth achieving.

67 The sentence is not so much the unit of thought but one unit of time and thus of thinking — a space similar to a day and subject to perhaps similar recurrences with slight differences (which yield to attention).

68 Ethical imperatives and questions probing moral efficacy occult only slightly in the shade of tonal ironizing.

69 As the day falls into place — certain forms allow for transmissiveness — on benches lunching.

70 Not a flemish interior but only looks so if glanced at rapidly; it is modern though its version of conflict is tender.

71 Must be one of my backward kinsmen who unabashedly takes a tan.

72 The level of integration in his work is as high as I have ever encountered, even as I allow for and admire its ironies, its inevitable incompleteness, its profound incapacities.

73 It is not a form of faith that predicates the least form of timelessness; it is an expression intensely retrograde and forward-looking, taking up temporary occupancy in the present.

74 His own (as my own) experiment, conducted in the framework of a more comprehensive failed national experiment, is doomed from the outset — either to fail outright or to give vent to a grating pumped compensatory optimism.

75 "I hold in my hand a Bonne Louise which is covered with minute brown specks or dots one twelfth to one sixteenth of an inch apart, largest and most developed on the sunny side, quite regular and handsome, as if they were the termination or operculum of pores which had burst in the very thin pellicle of the fruit, producing a slight roughness to the touch."

76 Sufficient analysis shows us to be in an increasingly complex (and thoroughly masked but definitively disempowering) web of financial forces; what then in this present work is that labor to which we are able?

77 "You would think it almost the labor of a lifetime for a tortoise to make its way from the surrounding shrubbery to this water, and how do they know that there is water here?"

78 "Geraniums bring thunder."

79 "I understand this response to *Walden* to be a boredom not of emptiness but of prolonged urgency."

80 "We are conversant with only one point of contact at a time, from which we receive a prompting and impulse and instantly press to a new season or point of conduct."

H's JOURNAL

3

June 22, 1990 – June 30, 1990

81 Though I hate equally the notions of intuition, inspiration, and imagination, know each to be fraudulent ad copy for self-aggrandizement, I myself work intensely (and best) by principles only partially known, at work by a method at once constructed and resistant to formulation.

82 "Far behind me they rest without bursting."

83 The movement of the text from the one written at home to that complicated social and financial negotiation which may result in a published product is often a deliberately neglected setting and season, attention being directed to a more pleasing vista at hand.

84, "What's the matter?"

85 These longish sentences display a tropism of sorts, a turning toward (and into) summer's long days of extended light and heat.

86 "It got up alarmed and trotted about on its long large legs, and even nibbled a little grass, and behaved altogether as if it had been an inhabitant of this planet for some years at least."

87 As I do theoretically (which is inseparable from breathing), I study the roots of St. Augustine to determine whether it is a fungus or cinch bugs responsible for the brown patches.

88 "America's best writers have offered one another the shock of recognition but not the faith of friendship, not daily belief."

89 The azaleas long done; still a few hydrangeas; plenty of day lilies — mainly orange or yellow — and this day, against an unusual (for here this time of year) blue sky: blasts of crepe myrtle's fuchsia blossoms.

90 "They get three cents apiece for them, not boiled."

91 The mayor of Tuscaloosa stands by his proclamation that city workers may not microwave popcorn in the Municipal Government Building: the seat of power shall not be made to smell like a movie theater.

92 "I feel that I am there only by sufferance; but I love to go by the villages by my own road, seeing them from one side, as I do theoretically."

93 Adam (or is it atom?), I name the plants and animals, I name all manner of things; but the names overlap, and some sound the same & give way to puns and play, and anyway I love nicknames, and to change names (as time passing yields other perspectives); so what is it that I am mapping?

94 "Where I turned up to go to Scusset village I saw some handsome patches of *Hudsonia tomentosa* (not yet had seen the *ericoides*), its fine bright-yellow flowers open chiefly about the edges of the hemispherical mounds."

95 When what is being described does not yet have being, then the language of description becomes another thing.

96 "The piping plover, as it runs half invisible on the sand before you, utters a shrill peep on an elevated key (different birds on different keys), as if to indicate its locality from time to time to its kind, or it utters a succession of short notes as it flies low over the sand or water."

97 There is a different sheen to sticky leaves of a pecan tree or shiny awkwardly large magnolia leaves when viewed in an era of stockpiled nuclear weaponry.

98 "Anyone who can speak can say the words, 'Thus saith the Lord,' as God is always finding out."

99 The sureness of the sentence, even as it confesses doubts, lies.

100 "In a genuine Cape Cod road you see simple dents in the sand, but cannot tell by what kind of foot they were made, the sand is so light and flowing."

101 To travel or to voyage, a journey, as a means of settling oneself; to theorize, as a going away and a returning to, but changed; such are the allegations, though the same might be claimed for staying put.

102 "War is like art because it must deal with calibrated space and the conflicts of partisans."

103 At some point the morning yields to the afternoon, and the writing of such sentences — until late in the evening — becomes impossible.

104 "Everything he can list he is putting in his book; it is a record of losses."

105 As if the regard, literally the attention, of one for another made the former feel substantial, important, worthy; so, nearly two-year-old Alan says, "I *told* you."

106 Once we abandon the notion that we must make the reader say "wow" or "awww," then we have, in spite of the loaded words, entered into — well, precisely through and in those words — a mature relationship, one of more sustained attention, in advent of the freight of such particular words, an adventure we may now embark upon.

107 "See apparently a young bobolink fluttering over the meadow."

108 The flickering of moth or junebug at the lefthand edge of my field of vision, sensation not unlike what I anticipate as a return of attention to this sentence a few years later — dim recognition of my participation in it, a vaguely familiar somewhat off-rhymed inhabitation of it — awash in a broadening and oddly comforting forgetfulness (which sometimes we are foolish enough to call progress or development).

109 Is it system per se, and its visibility ahead of time, that converts idle and attentive activity into work; and is the mystification of not-knowing anything other than the guarantee of an invisible harness?

110 RETURN UNBOUND JOURNALS HERE

111 To read in many (   ) at once.

112 It is difficult to remember when a dream, an ideal, a way of living presented itself as purely inviting (and I, or something that goes by such a name, assented to this one).

113 "In his youth his temperament was fiery and so to correct this he adopted measures."

114 He sits, comforted to think nothing needs doing right now.

115 Next door in curlers seventy-five year old Maree totters about and inspects where city workers removed underbrush from the far end of her yard, tells me she feels sicker than ever and in an hour or so she's to throw a party for a friend's eighty-fifth birthday, says she just prays to the good lord that she doesn't fall out; soon, the street fills with large white parked cars.

116 Time cannot be thought but can be thought about, or thought in, while thinking gives some compass to it, and even a particular pace and spin.

117 I am writhing ajournal; surely it could be verse.

118 Sings Alan after supper: "row row row your goat   gently down the street   merrily merrily merrily merrily   life is but a dream."

119 "What happens instead is that men mythologize their forces, as they always have, project them onto demigods, and then serve projections."

120 I write with no anxious grasping after: sooner or later, what I am doing will come to me.

H's JOURNAL

4

July 1, 1990 – July 29, 1990

121 "The river is now whitened with the down of the black willow, and I am surprised to see a minute plant abundantly springing from its midst and greening it, — where it has collected in denser beds against some obstacle as a branch on the surface, — like grass growing in cotton in a tumbler."

122 I think that our emotional lives — the breakthroughs, insights, honest confrontations, moments of sharing & vulnerability — are as thoroughly governed by their form as advertizing or the news or political speeches — each an achievement of a preordained desire by means of a rut-worn rhetoric; hold out, wait, and work for something else.

123 "Church and State and the Academy and Poetry and the City may each suppress philosophy, but they cannot, without its complicity, replace it."

124 A place made by the deliberate fronting of fact — the labor, deliberate, attentive work by hand, day-labor — to sojourn, that is, to take a day's journey within the sinewy twists of a sentence's expressive current — *that* currency passing as fact.

125 In relation to the Bay Area, I am on the verge of being able to say that I have had to go twenty years and two thousand miles away in order to be able to take another step comfortably in that direction; such is the distance from San Jose to Berkeley or Green Gulch.

126 Would Willie be pleased with her gifts — a panda bear fan and a magnetic refrigerator starfish — and are such designations somehow more a part of the world of facts than certain other words?

127 Within each sentence — but not this one — well, maybe — a narrative with its own particular twists and a moment of arrest.

128 "Love what is good as if bumping into furniture."

129 And then there is this other thing — a friend's voice from Illinois early in the morning; Matthew Brady's photographs of Andersonville prisoners; something horrendous blocking the procession of an extended catalog.

130 "Though I peered in at his eyes I could not discern myself reflected therein."

131 As with a serious head cold, perhaps the result of a virus born aloft by our ever running air conditioning system, so too the gray overcast day, within which I walk from the office to the library, much like a squirrel fallen from a tree branch, stunned, walking again as a means of waiting for the return of a determined grid of vision, wherein haste and orientation become falsely synonymous with vitality.

132 "But the *worker* has the misfortune to be a *living* capital, and therefore a capital *with needs* — one which loses its interest, and hence its livelihood, every moment it is not working."

133 Says the stutter is the plot — bumps up against the — the stops, valleys between whole numbers — a persistent abyss — a quiet hiss, generative, and then again & again: not.

134 "This broad field which I have looked at so long looks not to me as the principal cultivator, but away from me to influences more genial to it, which water and make it green."

135 , "if you finish all of your cereal, you will grow up to be as strong as an ambulance and as fast as a firetruck."

136 Many a different unit may function as poetry's building block, and from Ron and his grandmother Gertrude I have learned to consider the sentence as such a one; therefore, here & in this instance (of my fortieth year), I build my dwelling so, gauging as I go the depth, variety, continuity, and autonomy possible unto each.

137 "Yet not the less, in my case, did I think it worth my while to weave them, and instead of studying how to make it worth men's while to buy my baskets, I studied how to avoid the necessity of selling them."

138 One form of viral communication with the mid-nineteenth-century is a tendency to moralize.

139 "Labor produces not only commodities: it produces itself and the worker as a *commodity* — and this in the same general proportion in which it produces commodities."

140 Having lived for a time now in the presence of several good sentences, I have, by these guidelines, determined to labor in a way appropriate to a fine point pen, a folded over piece of scrap paper, and a stolen half hour hidden in the government documents room.

141 Quit the chit-chat, and cut to the chase.

142 "No method nor discipline can supersede the necessity of being forever on the alert."

143 Some said he labored in obscurity, to which he replied that such description trafficked in gross misconception; some said that she labored in obscurity, and feeling the sting of that neglect she, and a substantial group of others, fought to change her situation.

144 "I would preserve purity in act and thought, as I would cherish the memory of my mother."

145 After the (bullethole) period at the end of the sentence — sometimes deepening of attention, a rapt echoic dwelling, othertimes a turning away — then your journey commences.

146 "Methinks I am less thoughtful than I was last year at this time."

147 Sure, I had taken decongestants & antibiotics & had just finished teaching the Thoreau seminar so the room was spinning a little anyway & it was late Friday & I was tired, but this boy, six or seven years old (& this is not the-old-socrates-thing) had an amazing face, such eagerness to know, I guess he was deaf, his eyes were so liquid eager blue, he even had a touch of (what would have been a literary cliche) spittle on his chin, too exuberant a smile, such enthusiasm, that I am now dumbstruck and a little embarrassed, for I couldn't even summon the courage to ask his attentive mother what gives, what's the boy's story.

148 "If you stand right fronting and face to face to a fact, you will see the sun glimmer on both its surfaces, as if it were a cimeter, and feel its sweet edge dividing you through the heart and marrow, and so you will happily conclude your mortal career."

149 Some sentences must be written out — e.g., I am in exile here — in order to realize that what they state is now out-dated or altogether not so.

150 "The medieval proverb *nulle terre sans seigneur* [there is no land without its lord] is thereby replaced by that other proverb, *l'argent n'a pas de maitre* [money knows no master], wherein is expressed the complete domination of dead matter over mankind."

151 I wish there were something else to do when I talk speculatively and stammer than to have my eyes dart upward and all over the place.

152 "You can even detect a water-bug (*Gyrinus*) ceaselessly progressing over the smooth surface a quarter of a mile off; for they furrow the water slightly, making a conspicuous ripple bounded by two diverging lines, but the skaters glide over it without rippling it perceptibly."

153 A & I ambled down into a dry lily pond bed, poked around among damp weeds & curled up pads, shook black-balled seeds from flat open-handed pods, broke open a lily stalk & marvelled at the sticky white liquid bubbling up its eight concentric veins, did this in Moundville, Alabama, one of the southernmost sites for Indian mounds, then climbed up a ceremonial mound to find the rigged up display closed — once all this would have been pretense for a poem; but one of us moves in that time where such matters flatten out & correspondence and hyped up descriptions are precisely the things one no longer cares to believe in.

154 "Where there is considerable division of labor it is most difficult for the worker to direct his labor into other channels."

155 But, utopian as it may sound, anti-transcendentalism — resistance to the sentimentality inextricable from selectivity — has its own inherent limitations too: one, the finite nature of the journal itself, and two, anti-selectivity not only annihilates the preciosity of the lyric but also brings death to the poem itself, rendering written mediation superfluous.

156 "Taxed for having a soul, a ratable soul."

157 "We talked of rude and simple times, when men sat about large fires in cold bracing weather, with clear heads; and when other dessert failed, we tried our teeth on many a nut which wise squirrels have long since abandoned, for those which have the thickest shells are commonly empty."

158 Since the words themselves are commonly held, and since pen and paper, relatively speaking, are a common possession, it would appear reasonable to claim that this deed itself — except for the more limited partnership of a construction site and its complex regulations & difficult permits — is a joint enterprise.

159 "I wished to live, ah! as far away as a man can think."

160 "In that direction my windows commanded an unobstructed view of a lofty brick wall, black by age and everlasting shade, which wall required no spy-glass to bring out its lurking beauties, but for the benefit of all near-sighted spectators, was pushed up to within ten feet of my window panes."

H's JOURNAL

5

July 29, 1990 – August 28, 1990

161 "Shall we forever resign the pleasure of construction to the carpenter?"

162 A hammer and a saw: a capital and a period.

163 There are, finally, only a few such words — or sentences — which prove of such sustenance as you & I are seeking.

164 "Each of these little ruptures, so to call them, is in form a star with five rays; so that, if the apple is higher-colored, reflecting the sun, on the duller surface of this pear the whole firmament with its stars shines forth."

165 It was such a shock to see in her, to see manifest, a fresh quality of belief — though such is precisely her profession, her line of work, though most in it quite simply have it not in the least.

166 "Innumerable little streams overlap and interlace one with another, exhibiting a sort of hybrid product, which obeys half way the law of currents, and half way that of vegetation."

167 It *should* be the evening of her triumph, this office which exhibits the sum of her learning & being, part performance but best when also resisting that element, for the sake of itself.

168 It could be, as well it might, preliminary windings, stuck in, trying to, that the texture, of this time.

169 "It is difficult to begin without borrowing, but perhaps it is the most generous course thus to permit your fellow-men to have an interest in your enterprise."

170 In studying & theorizing this installation, I find myself mulling over memory as it is exhibited, lose myself, am stalled, maybe idling & then flooded (but enough of that), puzzle over the jars displaying objects found in an abandoned house — how to dwell with these particulars, to know them (as they are) without in the least making them mine.

171 Funny to turn a principally declarative unit into a span of time, a dwelling place, lyricism's very home (proclaimed the cuckoo).

172 Picante sauce, cilantro, jalapeño, pepper sauce, ginger root, crushed garlic: spies incur across the tongue's budded territories.

173 I don't know which you are (he said in his inseparable tone, a mixture of endearing & annoying, the risking of a view that others hazard not) frantically efficient or slowly growing; so, for your sixtieth birthday, I give you, mother, a hummingbird feeder and a bonsai tree.

174 I had maintained that visionary or mystic capability (as a fairly steady access) into my mid-thirties; I do not (but sometimes) lament its passing.

175 "And I discovered that when I put my hand on the mullein leaves they felt decidedly warm, but the radical leaves of the goldenrods felt cold and clammy."

176 I must get my hands on those sentences I wrote the other day and stuffed inside some book I was reading at the time.

177 Then came a whole flood of sentences, what I jokingly referred to as a whole month's work.

178 Is this nature writing which does without much in the way of trees, neither factual nor allegorical, and has little precision of (external) description?

179 We belong to a new & unusual group of artists: we *know* what we are doing.

180 "The echo is, to some extent, an original sound, and therein is the magic and charm of it."

181 "Yesterday I came here to live."

182 The roof is new, the wiring sound, so I suppose this house will do.

183 "Staying in the house breeds a sort of insanity always."

184 I respect office hours and will go to see her, seeking a blessing or the study of one sentence from the Torah, for such are her offices.

185 "It is only the serious eye peering from and the sincere life passed within it, which restrain laughter and consecrate the costume of any people."

186 : "Will is uphill still."

187 It took months to read that one.

188 He may be mistaken in assuming anger to be a fit conduit or in assuming that once anger subsides a residual tide of insightful words will enter in or in assuming that the word "or" has any validity as a discriminatory signpost.

189 "Many of these are drifted in amid the button-bushes, willows, and other shrubs, and the sedge, along the riverside, and the water falling just at this time, when they have put forth little fibres, they are deposited on the mud just left bare in the shade, and thus probably a great many of them have a chance to become perfect plants."

190 It is her fate to teach — and do it well, with passion — in a place where the parents instinctively fear and hate her; with the intensity of the tissue rejection phenomenon in an organ transplant, they will not let her help their children grow healthy with questioning.

191 "When a spring has been allowed to fill up, to be muddied by cattle, or, being exposed to the sun by cutting down the trees and bushes, to dry up, it affects me sadly, like an institution going to decay."

192 That what I do & the anxieties attendant upon said activity matters nought to him is but one point of tangency in the peculiarly divergent temporality of a father's love for his son.

193 "As I walked through the pasture side of the hill, saw a mouse or two glance before me in faint galleries in the grass."

193 "As I walked through the pasture side of the hill, saw a mouse or two glance before me in faint galleries in the grass."

194 When hit by a stick or a rock, by one or by several, most any metal object becomes a good drum.

195 "The trumpet-weed is already as high as my head, with a rich glaucous bloom on its stem."

196 He grumbles & he fulminates; can any sentence on its own (is there such a thing?) account for & enumerate in full its specific circumstances, as this one, written early on the morning of Monday, August 27, 1990, during the quiet of a power outage, with an inexpensive blue ballpoint pen in tiny script on a folded in half piece of white paper, my butt upon a nice blue & white striped chair (perhaps a recovered Queen Anne), Alan still asleep, Jane already off to teach the dreaded first day of a new school year, another hazy warm day in a month of oppressively dry such days — but this could go on and on and never acquire the precision of, say, missile coordinates, nor would it (as yet) have included a picture of George Bush playing golf & fishing in Maine while he puzzles over how to best Saddam Hussein at the game of oil, troops, nerve gas, hostages, and brinksmanship — and is this now a complete sentence?

197 "The events attending the fall of Dr. Johnson's celebrated willow at Lichfield, — a *Salix Russelliana* twenty-one feet in circumference at six feet from the ground, — which was blown down in 1829, were characteristic of the Briton, whose whole island, indeed, is a museum."

198 Whether this could be, is, and can be said — god, the stammer too becomes a masterable rhetoric — not the naivete of a coming to consciousness, but the making of a thing sister to what is.

199 “Near the point of each forward wing, a round black spot or eye, with a bluish crescent within its forward edge, and beyond this spot, a purple tinge with a short whitish waving line continued through it from the crescent.”

200 Tonight the tilted half moon exhibits a reddish tint — (and in these sentences where [and such as] we are) an infinity of interpretations.

H's JOURNAL

6

August 28, 1990 – October 26, 1990

201 "I sometimes awake in the night and think of friendship and its possibilities, a new life and revelation to me, which perhaps I had not experienced for many months."

202 I felt, perhaps incorrectly, that until that moment we had been, as a small group of men meeting for nearly four years, without testiness, so my own abrasive & impertinent remark could not, with whatever amount of acquired southern politeness, ever be cleanly papered over.

203 "The place they had thoughts on was some of the vast and unpeopled countries of America, which are fruitful and fit for habitation, being devoid of all civil inhabitants, where there are only savage and brutish men which range up and down, little otherwise than the wild beasts of the same."

204 All it would take would be a lot of money, and then I could

205 "For summer being done, all things stand upon them with a weather-beaten face, and the whole country, full of woods and thickets, represented a wild and savage hue."

206 Such is the history of my relationships to groups: either a timidity that precludes my ever beginning or an intensity & expectation — depth of my own need? — that soon wrecks and makes edgy what otherwise had been reasonably fine.

207 "In the meantime, the Pequots, especially in the winter before, sought to make peace with the Narragansetts, and used very pernicious arguments to move them thereunto: as that the English were strangers and began to overspread their country, and would deprive them thereof in time, if they were suffered to grow and increase."

208 Each must earn a living; therefore, each September we fall.

209 "It was a fearful sight to see them thus frying in the fire and the streams of blood quenching the same, and horrible was the stink and scent thereof; but the victory seemed a sweet sacrifice, and they gave the praise thereof to God, who had wrought for them, thus to enclose their enemies in their hands and gave them so speedy a victory over so proud and insulting an enemy."

210 But if, as I believe, tension proves instructive, then of course avoid the genial practice of the already known.

211 "*Savory expressions* using to breath *from compunct and broken Hearts*, and a sence of *inward hardnesse* and *unbrokennesse*."

212 Could these be then as an investigation but without accompanying explanation?

213 "He wanted runners to go and seek the smoke of the council fire."

214 And so on any given morning, only a finite amount of correspondence may be extended — and then settle in and wait for its return.

215 "Specimens of spicery were intrusted to them that they might judge if anything similar existed in the country."

216 The editor of *Art Seller* had moved to San Diego to direct a corporate art gallery (whence she was seized with the idea for her magazine); she spoke eloquently of the difficult market (prior to the advent of her publication) for the private collector who suddenly expresses an interest in serious deacquisition.

217 "I suffered nothing to be touched, and went with my captains and some of the crew to view the country."

218 For it seems to me that an oppositional consciousness may in fact be one that, in its own way, seeks adulation by sensing, and leading, through articulation, a turning in the tide; and thus it is a danger — this ability to feel chiefly in opposition — if & as one is profoundly or even superficially wrong about a change in the climate of one's time.

219 "So great were the fear and distraction of these people, some to reach us sooner than others, that they might touch us, they pressed us so closely that they lacked little of killing us; and without letting us put our feet to the ground, carried us to their dwellings."

220 It settled upon him at around age forty, without appreciable regret: the taciturn act of being, without apology, himself.

221 "On no account would we consent that they should rejoice over us any more that night."

222

223 After quite some silence, and some sickness, sentences begin again to come to me.

224 It is as into — no; skip the *as* — a world of intense caring.

225 Reprieve deprive private complex stutter rhyme stress clot complete.

226 "Mrs. H___, being removed to the Isle of Aquiday, in the Narragansett Bay, after her time was fulfilled, that she expected deliverance of a child, was delivered of a monstrous birth, which, being diversely related in the country, (and in the open assembly at Boston, upon a lecture day, [was] declared by Mr. Cotton to be twenty-seven several lumps of man's seed, without any alteration or mixture of anything from the woman, and thereupon gathered that it might signify her error in denying inherent righteousness, but that all was Christ in us, and nothing of ours in our faith, love, etc.)."

227 He had come upon the sentence as a migratory — temporal & spatial — occasion; that, white, he plopped himself down in a rundown meat & three lunch place — TinTop — in the west end, black, of town and listened and wrote (but not exactly this).

228 "And when the discourse was ended, I walked abroad alone, in a solitary place in my father's pasture, for contemplation."

229 The desire to be understood is adolescent in its nature, and must fade away, or give rise to anger, frustration, and recurrent — adolescent — outbursts lamenting what cannot be, and certainly what cannot, by lamentation, be made to happen.

230 Chimney swifts and in some instances bats flutter and dart at sunset this Sunday, & with the loss of light, weekly, my spirits sink.

231 "The difficulty consists in the manner of viewing so extensive a scene."

232 My brother was exceptional, and no one liked him very much; so what was the point?

233 Persistent attempts at self-declaration have value as they collide with one another.

234 "Used often-times to dwell long on one sentence, to see the wonders contained in it; and yet almost every sentence seemed to be full of wonders."

235 In spite of his desire to ground all writing in its material circumstances, in spite of his desire to situate the written within specific modes of production, his experience of these sentences was principally as a series of sporadic and unbeckoned transmissions.

236 Some ridiculousness entails, some twisting of time, in allying mid-nineteenth century and present instances of deference, transgression, indirection, violent boldness, private writing, and the mismatches of commercial publishing.

237 When I had described the girl standing with toes pointed out, a sort of informal ballet position, I had meant to suggest that walking and standing are culturally determined — even over-determined — actions, gestures learned to please others and to present practiced images of submission, strength, and alluring vulnerability; thus is beauty truth.

238 "Memorandum. This rampant hag, Martha Carrier, was a person of whom the confessions of the witches, and of her own children among the rest, agreed that the devil had promised her she should be Queen of Hebrews."

239 By the sheer ardency of his desire for justice, he had separated himself from his kind: "writers   who as writers   cannot afford to be part of any nation"

240 "Whenever the waters are exhausted and the seeds are exhausted you will send us prayer sticks."

H's JOURNAL

7

November 15, 1990 – January 6, 1991

241 As if the mirrors & the mall could be anywhere — they cannot — and this disinterestedness were also unbound; but the — a or this — sentence too is not natural (though it might be the most natural thing in the world to jot it down just so).

242 Surely as the better dressed move determinedly back & forth — *it is not meant as criticism to note the neatness of their dress?*

243 A greater percentage of men than women talking to themselves.

244 The collection of sentences stood suggestive: an array to go back to & perhaps do something with.

245 It is hard to tell who is doing (the) work around here.

246 The instance, the specific circumstance, of writing rarely gets mentioned, as if it were assumed to be neutral or not of interest, though in this sentence, written in a white plastic chair outdoors in Tampa (when should this specificity break off) in a brickcourtyard in the city center esplanade, my means of evasion (of the convention & badges & sessions nearby), this my way this hot November day to intensify.

247 Some are indeed hurrying, but the colors of the esplanade are not conducive to it.

248 Churn out / cram in: one more sentence as the sun sets.

249 It dawns on me that Mary's captivity narrative moves from one enclosure to another: domesticity (husband, children, kitchen), to the natives' shifting encampment & varying forms of servitude, and then back home again.

250 "Our moulting season, like that of the fowls, must be a crisis in our lives."

251 When his father becomes understood as disappointing, the young man then learns to love his mother (whom he had formerly viewed through his father's beleaguered eyes) and understands his own strength as derived from hers; then begins a slow reconciliation with and revision of his father — this story a common one for men of my generation.

252 Of Emily I am still — Dazzled — and have no — Distance.

253 Only from the perspective of my having quit it does it get named "a huge waste of my time" — though the convenience, indeed the automaticness, of that description leaves me suspicious.

254 Do not, my dear friends, (overly) professionalize your literary life.

255 "Faith is Doubt," she wrote; and what can be my possible relations to her utterance?

256 In America now the story has changed from the incomplete, the land & people of endless promise, that expansive restlessness, to we are finishing up, we are about done, we are finished.

257 Suicide may be understood as occupying a moral high ground: if you reject "work in order to be free," you may also reject "choose so that you may be chosen."

258 At a certain point, the diary presents itself as female.

259 Immediately after disaster, she says the question is Avalanche or Avenue.

260 Crucial weights differ, if they do, as Syllable and Sound.

261 I cannot tell you that what is accomplished here conforms to metric X or metric Y; but I hereby do swear that it be attuned with what care I can muster, and music (of new sorts) remains a going concern.

262 "The conditions for poetry rest outside each life at a miraculous reach indifferent to worldly chronology."

263 "Amazing human heart, a syllable can make to quake like jostled tree, what infinite for thee?"

264 "In some sense the subject of any poem is the author's state of mind at the time it was written."

265 Simple retrospect allows me to speculate that our nation's early absorption in & fascination with captivity narratives does portend our currently fading but still exercised skill as a supreme capturer of global resources.

266 "Already worrying about the metaphysical puzzle of time, she knew by instinct what most of us take years to learn, that time lived forward is only understood backward, that social existence merely negates spiritual progress."

267 "In each human being, things are constantly shifting in their significance, as is the underlying neurophysiological response."

268 "Driven by enormous intellectual ambition into the vicinity of the mutilated message of all poetry, they fear the failure of their own energy."

269 Parents are understood (if ever) in retrospect.

270 "She carries intelligence of the past into future of our thought by reverence and revolt."

271 One must imagine and then make a poetry in keeping with time as one has it.

272 "My precursor attracts me to my future."

273 She continues to be ingenious & fully generative; one could speak of the paths of grasshoppers, those abstractionists, on hot afternoons; or of ice melting upon a warm stovetop; or the fragrance of metal; or better yet her, and perhaps thus our, ability in absolute intensification — to sustain no anxious grasping after.

274 The missing term is certainty.

275 Himself rejected again and again in ways that brought with it considerable pain, he withheld from others his own approval, as if that approval were something just.

276 I was in my young adulthood (with all the attendant gender stupidities of this assertion) virtually a daily stalker after spirit.

277 If I read her right — it's all a thinking in.

278 Turning herself in — inward — already held captive by authorities against whom there was virtually no other way to resist, she placed herself under the command of other figures, in whose hands her own governance was more permissible.

279 "You noticed my dwelling alone — To an Emigrant, Country is idle except it be his own."

280 "Perhaps Death — gave me awe for friends — striking sharp and early, for I held them since — in a brittle love — of more alarm, than peace."

H's JOURNAL

8

January 9, 1991 – March 2, 1991

281 It's not so much a matter of representing silence but of respecting and acknowledging that which is not writing and that which prevents or impedes writing.

282 "Sky water."

283 Each entry performs a procedure by example, and so for the whole.

282 Here, today, January 13, 1991, it makes some sense to pause & consider the implications of what seems like our imminent precipitation of a war with Iraq, to say that war *looms*; indeed it does, many threads at once, as Russians murdered Lithuanians yesterday, and war continues in Somalia, and within our own inequitable cities handgun violence stutters on, and it is not Russia or South Africa that has the highest per capita percentage of its citizens in jail, but us, and it is time again for our makers of sophisticated weaponry to have a "live" chance to test and enhance the value of their products — and so thoughts of a looming war must be interwoven with a daily meditation on the intensity of violence and dissatisfaction which already is our daily bread.

285 "The maggot in their heads is patriotism."

286 "The bullet of your thought must have overcome its lateral and ricochet motion and fallen into its last and steady course before it reaches the ear of the hearer, else it may plough out again through the side of his head."

287 How could she read this aloud, so loudly does it already call in its unnameable way, disorder being one side of the story, defiance (and the harassed ways of a new faith) being another.

288 "Deliver me from a city built on the site of a more ancient city, whose materials are ruins, whose gardens cemeteries."

289 When I wrote these pages, or rather the bulk of them, I lived alone, in a study, a room removed from the rest of my family, in a house which my wife and I were slowly paying off, in The Downs, in Tuscaloosa, Alabama, and earned my living by the ambiguous and indefinite labor of reading, writing, and conversing.

290 My writing career has been a process of learning to write in ways I had not yet read before; thus, time after time, I have immediately achieved an audience, and in the process shed the prospects of one.

291 "To regret deeply is to live afresh."

292 One technique, or fundamental methodology, which I am quite attracted to, & which may bear some resemblance to a sustained composition by difference (CB?), is a sustained resistance to refinement of a style.

293 "With thinking we may be beside ourselves in a sane sense."

294 How easily we accommodate ourselves to war — especially when waged at a distance, with our news releases carefully filtered, and, as is often the case, when we drop bombs on people of dark or different skin tones — though once a groundwar starts we may have to readjust, and of course we can, and learn to take in stride more immediate instances of casualties, some of whom look remarkably like ourselves.

295 "Keep your distance, do not infringe on the interval between us, and I will pick up lime and lay real terrestrial eggs for you, and let you know by cackling when I have done it."

296 A strategy of specific circumvention of a typical (journal-istic) visual orientation — such erasure performed upon this site — leaves other objects present for attention: *this*, and *these*.

297 "The whole cut impressed me as if it were a cave with stalactites laid open to the light."

298 This is the one story I can tell; and it is not one.

299 "From the repeated critical impulses to understand Thoreau by looking away from his own work, one would have to acknowledge that something about his writing barricades itself against investigation."

300 One mystery of transmission: I am JB Murry holding a small bottle of holy water before mystic script; though I wrote it, I require this agency (and must look through it) to resolve my own scrawl.

301 "I am not thou; thou art not I."

302 To bring into presence by way of words things which do not answer to our ways of knowing, to make alluring and engaging instances of such, that would be a good work of knowing, labor worth playing with.

303 "I am not so poor: I can smell the ripening apples; the very rills are deep; the autumnal flowers, the *Trichostema dichotomum* — not only its bright blue flower above the sand, but its strong wormwood scent which belongs to the season — feed my spirit, endear the earth to me, make me value myself and rejoice; the quivering of pigeons' wings remind me of the tough fibre of the air which they rend."

304 It dawned on me today why they had reacted so badly to Cavell's word "scripture" for *Walden*: I am a Jew and they are Christians (or retired versions thereof), so "scripture" to me does not mean a fixed text to be worshipped in absolute subordination — instead, a generative site, a beginning, holy & open to a great range of interplay.

305 "Our choice is not between belief and unbelief, but between faith and idolatry — whether we will be metaphysicians or manikins."

306 How can you stand to continue to look at it and not do anything?

307 "Every sentence is the result of a long probation."

308 Often, though I wish it were not so, my reading experience remains flat, lifeless, obligatory, and uninspiring; yet, strangely, a discussion of it the next morning may completely resurrect that reading, yielding new insights and producing in me an unaccountable enthusiasm, so that what had been, against my will, a dull text returns a treasure raised from a wreck thought unreachable.

309 "It is so rare that we see a large body self-sustained in the air."

310 Missing from these daily formulations, and from most sentences especially of the declarative variety, is the intensity of struggle and conflict, the drift of cross-purposes, the hazardous (social) act of claiming "one's own time" or even a seeming of oasis of such within a day's already erected or thrown obligations, entanglements present and consented to that surround and disturb (but perhaps also make possible, as irritation a pearl) these written habitations.

311 "The value of the experiment is that it does give you experience of an interval as between one life and another — a greater space than you ever travelled."

312 What such books project — or, rather, essay as our fit project — is a lyricism of reading.

313 "There were prophets, but there is no Zion; knowing that, Jesus fulfilled them, but the kingdom of heaven is not entered into; knowing that, the Founding Fathers brought both testaments to this soil, and there is no America; knowing that, Jonathan Edwards helped bring forth a Great Awakening, and we are not awake."

314 I would need to write that sentence which fit here if I knew for certain what that meant; even so, I suspect that dusk, steady rain, minor flooding, a mention of February 22nd 1991, & anticipation of tomorrow's visit from Jerry & Diane would also figure in.

315 "The act of thinking, Thoreau would maintain, specifically the act of thinking about nature, requires tolerating the very confusions and contradictions the *Journal* — in explicit terms — sees itself replicating."

316 In blunting the aphoristic drift of these sentences, various resources come into play — humor, interrogation, deliberate flatness, extended description, and so forth; nevertheless, the aphoristic asserts itself quite stubbornly as if it were the landlord of these premises and were meant to hold sway here.

317 "The problems to which I point apply to quotation of any literary text — to quotations of any text at all — but the *Journal's quite specific features make the ordinary liabilities of excerption seem to preclude its proper representation.*"

318 Must it justify itself by being in a fixed and recognizable form, as if to assure us of its (nondecomposing) definiteness?

319 The storm, the pressure, the pressure in his chest, the desk, a list, his little boy, the storm, the pressure, the pressure in his chest.

320 "We need to witness our own limits transgressed, and some life pasturing freely where we never wander."

H's Journal

9

March 29, 1991 - July 12, 1991

321 "Each Consciousness must emigrate/ And lose its neighbor once — "

322 "More numerous of Windows" would be one way to number (& not benumb) the difference, to assess the distance, to survey the expanse of such captivity: what I might call a sentence.

323 It is odd, and the way, til now, that I have been; but I now feel myself rushing into the world, not that I am what one would call "at home" in the world, but it feels exactly right, as if it is my particular turn to be here, to leave behind some field of solitude & spend accumulated learning, to enter into a world of routine social interaction, oddly enough with an all but vanished sense of irony and distance.

324 "The Mind is so near itself — it cannot see, distinctly — and I have none to ask — "

325 A reading of *A Succession of Forest Trees* explains why prose, here, after this period of dwelling, gets supplanted by a more lyrical version (of poetry), how this consideration of seeds, dissemination, and replacement gets taken over by hers of lightning, dashes, and the inexplicable.

326 "To escape enchantment, one must always flee."

327 Never arriving, there are asymptotes we edge toward; then there is the one we would *like* to think so — but we do get there, in time.

328 "Perhaps Affection has always one question more which it forgot to ask."

329 "I know we shall certainly see what we loved the most."

330 "… there seems a spectral power in thought that walks alone — "

331 "I hope that nothing pains you except the pang of life, sweeter to bear than to omit."

332 "To come unto our own and our own fail to receive us, is a sere response."

333 This whole family feud: about how & where to care for Fanya (who at ninety-two probably *is* dying), but about (thereafter) how the living shall be known to one another.

334 What is poetry if not a kind of writing which requires perpetual readjustment of reading.

335 Susan, it's *not* that Johnson & Franklin were consciously malicious; their attempts to finalize & represent her writing simmered, & finally gave off a self-ironizing odor, with their ardor, *not* the order that they had desired.

336 "Then I take out the words I don't want."

337 "There is not only a vivid green halo about each spot, but the back is vivid light-green between the spots."

338 Mabel Loomis Todd on paper Q.

339 To write within a specific form, with(in) its own specific rigors, to do so decidedly & in such a manner that the writing resists becoming something.

340 "The males agree very well."

341 It is a sense of a brain, a whole specific being, an individual's accumulation of available language, being brought to bear in a particular interval of thinking.

342 Surviving Transcripts: World (purple) on paper Y.

343 Everything takes its toll — money, bad food, booze — so, he reasoned, no point in cushioning your body, or some illusion of a life, from that barrage.

344 To listen somewhat helplessly is all that I can do — our relation now reciprocal — mother & son — as I hear your troubles, your complaints, your pain of no money and fruitless hard work — for each of us has been and will be — victor and victim of circumstance.

345 "Washing the dishes, especially the greasy ones, is the most irksome duty of the camp, and it reminded me of that sacred band in Fourier's scheme, who took upon themselves the most disagreeable services."

346 "Never having travelled far from his hillside, he does not suspect himself, but tells his stories with fidelity and gusto to the minutest details, — as much as Herodotus his histories."

347 "To sit under the face of an old clock that has been ticking one hundred and fifty years, — there is something mortal, not to say immortal, about it!"

348 "'While you take in hand to school others, and to teach them by what name a whale-fish is to be called in our tongue, leaving out, through ignorance, the letter H, which almost alone maketh up the signification of the word, you deliver that which is not true.'" (*Hackluyt.*)

349 Yes, scarcity enacts revenge, except it succeed too well: then, delight & despair reside affixed in one body, and will may well have gone awry.

350 "Neither editor saw fit to point out the fact that Shepard left two manuscripts in one book separated by many pages then positioned them so that to read one you must turn the other upside down."

351 "This, then, is the way forests are planted."

352 "The written word is before us — apparently given in its totality by 'being before us' as the philosophers say — and its innocent appearance exploits our innocence."

353 "To my surprise, it allowed me to slide my hand under it and lift it up, while it squatted cold and moist in the middle of my palm, panting naturally."

354 "Standing on the edge of the wood and looking through it, — for it is quite level and free from underwood, *mostly* bare, red-carpeted ground, — you would have said that there was not a hardwood tree in it, young or old, though I afterward found on one edge a middling-size sassafras, a birch, a small tupelo, and two little scarlet oaks, but, what was more interesting, I found, on looking closely over its floor, that, alternating with thin ferns and small blueberry bushes, there was, as often as every five feet, a little oak, three to twelve inches high, and in one place I found a green acorn dropped by the base of a tree."

355 "My need — was all I had — I said," though timid am I to stage it or to say it, & need *for* what I cannot say, though I pray I may be upheld by another preposition: need *of* what — so this urge may be placed in the service of.

356 "The other worm, which was at first curled up still and emitted a duller light, was one and one twentieth inches in length and also showed two dots of light only on the forward segment."

357 "Glimpses do ye seem to see of that mortally intolerable truth; that all deep, earnest thinking is but the intrepid effort of the soul to keep the open independence of her sea; while the wildest winds of heaven and earth conspire to cast her on the treacherous, slavish shore?"

358 "Thought is the Knock which "

359 *Mis amigos*: earth & sky, mortals & divinities: a breath, a boat, a wave — goodbye; embark: *ola* halo hello *hola* — hail the silent *h*, distant kinsman of *aleph* — friend of the unsaid (goes unspoken) [ghost unspoken]; friend of the already said — gets reiterated, with (in) a difference.

360 "The break with the old world was a rupture into contraries."

H's Journal

10

October 19, 1991 - December 8, 1991

361 I could have become the bird (I heard) in song, the tree (I felt) arching over me, and I did not, and in that refusal I insist (as nonetheless I disappear) belongs the visionary and the contemporary lyric, an intensity which catches itself and must stay put in (tragically) material circumstances.

362 Confused by refusing the varied (buried?) splendor of our time — oh eyes (long pause), grow otherwise.

363 The year here falls on (— deaf ears —); now ninety-two she says some days are good days, some days are bad days; I tell her I could say the same; she says, "I pray each day I don't get any worse."

364 No quick fix in the sentence, a writer's fix-it shop; you could fix the game, as professional wrestling matches are fixed, but that would wreck it (at least for those for whom the outcome is misidentified as the game); or, you could affix your attention adhesively to play: the play within the sentence's mechanisms, the play's the thing, an adult returning to child's play with the serious intent of exuberant recovery, knowing no quick fix possible.

365 It is disheartening this time of grim money & of public scorn for education — when revelation or private ruminative space can break (in) and sustain — the nominative & generic drift, the pronoun's placement.

366 As a partitioning by difference, as an instance of attention, what length is a span, and how to make from it.

367 This was much after but somehow continuous with.

368 As for that other Henry, how could he write and write, hours every day, in a journal, and never mention the activity of writing, as if that scene of composition were not, as if that handiwork were not a part of nature, as if he himself were not a body on the scene; I write this October 25, 1991, in the mid-morning, in blue ink; I am dressed in gray slacks and a starched white shirt; I will not go to my other office for some time.

369 We marched, more than a thousand of us, and in that "we," difference, I white, and a few other whites among a thousand blacks, a silent candle-holding march, to face down blackface offensive acts.

370 Attention where, to the book in his lap, to the dick beneath sweatpants under the book, through the bay window to the bare dogwood or puffy pines — she is right: "our picaresque obsequiousness" — or the smell of sweet potatoes baking, cold feet and early daylight, stolen reading time, the little boy's mild snoring — which of these, which.

371 A clay pig in the shape of a dog; wall mural in a rural cafe: cows grazing in a green meadow but cows the shape of st. bernards.

372 The art critic grew bothered at the fact that this particular folk artist grew less and less naive, especially about the dollar value and commercial network of his paintings; each had been originally primitive, but the art critic more so, more steadily so, and certainly more monochromatically.

373 If the time were my own and the whole day like the early morning this journal would not consist of sentences.

374 We give thanks for the difficulties that may transform us, but never when they occur.

375 He had imagined the previous sentence as the beginning of an address to his relatives gathered for a holiday meal; now, he smiles at certain formal complexities of address, knowing that their imagined presence gives the imagined address immediacy while in actuality they are among those least likely ever to read the actual (and now oddly detached or differently placed) written sentence.

376 If it could be anything, any of the letters you have wished for, which one today would it be.

377 He had been steeped in a great tradition, & thus it never occurred to him that the English which he spoke and wrote was in fact not French or Italian and that to insist on coercing that American speech into regularized rhymes was simply a kind of cultural hangover, an old error carried forward, his unthinking repetition of a wrong turn based on envy and (l)imitation, & if he wasn't careful he would lose forever the particular grit, music, and invention urgent in his present American moment.

378 She had assembled an arsenal of satisfactory materials; she was ready to begin; she began, and the new work took shape.

379 How many of us, over an extended period, can work together well — two? three? four? five? six? seven?

380 Their dog cut his foot and bled on the new carpet; their little boy woke up three times in the middle of the night coughing and crying; it had been cold, rainy, and gray for a week; money, as always, was a problem; these are reasons why nature is not described these days in detail and why, unlike the all too present past tense and dull verb "to be," literarily appropriate moods of reverent attention and wonderful discovery are absent.

381 You were here now; leaves were mostly yellow and falling; I had no passport, and "China" was only an arresting word but not yet a place to go to.

382 I said to my wife, "and what about Lyn?"; she said, "nice; but she could use a little make up."

383 The gray dog had grown old, lost most of his eager to please intelligence, and become instead a stubborn and irritating test of the entire family's compassion.

384 Yes, I eat meat; yes, I eat fried foods; yes, I may use the term "christian" non-ironically.

385 More and more he begins to wish for those around him an easy death.

386 I was reading her Russian book, but here in Tuscaloosa not snow but heat or light or humidity falls about us, makes us stay put, takes away the urgency of any destination.

387 Ants or sanderlings or the nervous circular transformations of quartz-powered digits.

388 Without thinking much about it, he had chosen to live not with another artist but a normal woman with a gift for mimicry and bitterness, humor and no bullshit (though now he wonders about use of the pronoun "he" instead of "I," why the past tense if I'm writing now, and the insidious way that assonance governs his discoveries).

389 Every morning, the second sentence out of his mouth: "daddy, read me a story."

390 I like people's work whose work I have a chance to like.

391 If this university were run by african-americans, instead of restoring the president's mansion we might be locating unmarked graves of slaves and writing a new narrative telling who actually built the school and learning what their lives were like & what options were open.

392 Sincerity itself became irretrievably contaminated by its accepted means of expression; like realism, it requires reinvention — a task, I should add, rich in emotion.

393 "And what is it I want now from a book?" — and in her question he felt serious vistas of uncertainty and desire, restlessness and duty open up within him a sort of perpetual preface, a surface tension, a dancer trying to follow (or lead) a new partner, a rarely acknowledged but all important quizzical adhesiveness (that might someday become a principal subject of reading, and of critical expression).

394 "That too will be included in it" — "you mean, what I'm saying just now?" — "that too."

395 Somehow she'd evaded the typical alternation of plot & description, omitting both.

396 You too will say this is a conversation I can enter into.

397 It was one of those projects which when outlined can be imagined fully (though in each instance a little bit differently) by almost anyone: the invention of Yosemite, delimitation and designation of particular vistas as constituting Yosemite *per se,* this making scenic though vast sublime complex archaic, in descriptions and photographs, the collaborative definitions, John Muir and Ansel Adams, the mixed telling of massive granite planes and the essentializing force of large plate negatives for nature photography.

398 rap chant prophecy mad Pip jive streetboy marxist collisionist collage syllable word machinegun guitar spray

399 I ask you how it is we are together in this now.

400 Very funny the way this comes about.

NEGATION

for Charles Bernstein

in affirmation

by negation

Negation 1

Of interest each
Not so
Lying
Yes taken away

Beyond brought back made into behind
Yon

Levitate let alone into letdown
On
One won stuns stammers
Kind
Independence means
Nowhere
Gathering dispersed

To
How
Ends

Nub nuzzle back to nibble
Except as a form of regret
Good to meet a pronoun
Attitude
Towards
Invisibility
Vulnerable only as
Exceptions dealt with

In what sense
North was where and afterwards

Tendentious
Happenstance plinking harpsichord
Election regulations

Farm character national jeffersonian backbone
Ass bray okay who say
College collision
Endowment

Argent made urgent
Necropolis
Despite rescue efforts

Dilated ten centimeters
Well
Early warning systems
Lack
Lick
In all known instances
Nook
Ground breaking beef (hog) day

Wurlitzer
Ice encased branches
Thinking
Hastens obligation to

Ink
Towards

Negation 2

Brought back from
Unable
Then again

Torrential could be thought of
Hazard a
Executive

Last but not
In retrospect
Formative
Ears

Olden
Fell out with

Moreso
Insidious intent
Never having courted
Denial don't

Investigative
Suture

Not about to reveal
On the other hand
Tough and tiff aren't

Originally a member of
Next
Exactly as

Televisional
Hermeneutics
Around about
Thermal inversion

Since thinking is
Honk if hue
Underpinnings
Not exactly what
So

Death
Extemporizes
At
That
Held up pending

Addendum
Nor
Desecrate

Kin and kind must be kept within
Elohim
Elderberry
Perspective
Sensitive to

Closed quote
Leaped out of
Earlier
As the first greek thinkers
Recall

Order
Fountain

Destitute of
Earnest about
Sorry about
Thinking of
Really what was meant was
Unctious (unconscious)
Caution
Turn the other
Imprint
On the outs
None of

Negation 3

In
That it must however

End(ure)
Nothing like it
Despite
Unreasonableness from all parties concerned
Regardless of stated intentions
Euthanasian invitation
Sedimental mood

Declaration of (from)
Elbow room
Alleviate
Terminal degree
Heuristic (yoursister)

Anabaptist
Nor way
Deadly sons

In
No

Death
Extracts promises that
Allotropism is all over
Turn a
Hora the hora

Moan moan
And
Iteration can be lived with
Next to
Tabernacle knock on wood
And
Iteration can be lived with
Next to
Situated

Illustration
Title to (of)
Send a

Because
Elective surgery might
In spite of previous
Night after night
G

Negation 4

Th(is)at
Holiday and anyway
Elevates the rhetoric

Perhaps and
Of the exchange of n and g
Reminded that
That
Every vapor has
Not memory can recall
Too many never
Originates but is not original to
Unless and less
S

Portentous to portending
Over
Where learning is personal venture
Ensured
Recuper

Obviously some
For every

Tell the whole
How to knowhow and wherewithall
Embedded and better

Neatness
Exit wound
Ground under
All over this great
Turnip or thumbnail call to a halt
In vitro
Value as the surplus of
Enabling

Involved with
This and only this possible here

Isn't
Said

The trick
Hold on to the
Edge cutters

E words such as each and even
Not positive whether
Examples of
Remain as if romance were
Glib
Yard sale

Oregonian origami
Folded over

Thought it over and
Hurts came to the surface
Ontology all told
Urban briefcase backdrop
Gone underground
Had to show respect to
Thinking

Negation 5

Won through
Instances of
Notoriety
Selves (sands) rearranged

Tending
Or

Illustrations cast a pall
Threads threnodies
Sincerely or not at

Trunk haitian
Relapse
Ultimatum old tomato
Tintinnabulation
Hocum hiccups hocus

Well intentioned
Held out until
Elements of
Nincompoopism

Isaac means laughter
Turds droppings

Funnel
Instances of instantiation
Nowadays
Demeaning opportunity knocking
Since that

Incorrect (anything)
Terminal displays
Soon to be
Eclectic bottlecap collection
Liberty or
Fucking

Unless of course after
Tablets
Tables
Endtables end up beside sofas
Rhythm with respect to
Loping along
Yesterday proceeds as

Tell exactly the whole
Outlay
Reinscribed
Not as had been

Assault with a
So that intent remains debateable
Uppermost in
Nuthatch
Disguised as a
Entry level
Rubble

Negation 6

Talk
Has advantages
Initiation proceeds until
Slippery

Duck under but not duck over nor duck beside
W expresses concern about possible inauthenticity
Early but not so early as
Lapidary quality to repetition
Lilt as opposed to stiletto
Ink which
Not what
Groan up

Belgian waffles
Ermine
Silver
Ill gotten
Domino
European handling

Institute for
Tin ears

If the subject
Sister (of)

Temptations
Hysteria growing like wysteria
Exerts (or thinks about)

Many a
Alternate route
Garlic capital of
Insider trading
Common as

Power
Over
Weather
Endings
Require

Tributary
Harboring a
Autonomy vs. metonymy
Tribunal

Covert suppurations
Obtuse
Noninstrumental piano
Virginity
Ellipsis
Rhombus (pigmy hippopotamus)
Taxonomy
Subverts

The suburbs
Heartening observation
Elevation unknown

Neutral party
Elder statement
Great(er)est
Apparently without any
Turbulence unattributable to
Instinct
Verve
Exhume

In turn
Not as many as had been
Trotlines
Observation deck

By
Entirely
Imperceptibly
Neutrino enriched fictions
Godly dimensions

Negation 7

Manners
Any ten year old mode
Yearly variable

Rough (roux)
Egret sanctuary
Gonad development
Arteriosclerosis
Registered for
Desertion

Informant to a cormorant
Tic

Alleviates all
Survivalist cults

The automobile industry's safety standards committee
Hell calling 911
Early versions of the person

Detailed blueprints
Envelope on the
Finite (freckle) coordinates
Expanded memory
Curtain call
Torn into

Oxygen poor
Fervent anti

By not
Or
Then on the other
Hand

Oblivion zeroed in
Purchased the slightest of toe holds
Purchased a digital quartz watch
Own up to the fact
Sentiments turned against
In a manner of speaking
Terse
Endowed with (by)
Summit of the nonaligned

By a series of multidirectional relationships
Usually a right reserved
To

Implied
Triumph over

Intelligence and imagination conceptual amoeba
Splitting splitting returning

Trunc
Heav
En
In
Road

Versions of the earliest known
Exonerate
Remarkable for
Yet

Such obsessed with which lives being now language
Orthography under house arrest
Unguents forbidden
Licensing of language operators

Time's distribution and equilibrium
Hebrew letters
Elaborate
Irrational numbers raised to higher powers
Run of hearts

Mounting to new
Ontic pretenses
Via whatever
Involved interlocutor
Not until or unless
Guilt

Sensible requirement agreed upon
Percolates up
Irritant
Return of the (depressed)
In the guise (geist) of
Torment

Negation 8

Cannibal upon
Extraterrestrial
Report card
Tantamount to
Accusation of
Insistence upon
Negation as the only

Tuned to the heuristic
Howling and the folds fell open
Irreducible to
Nonacknowledgement of certain forces
Knowledge of such forces
Ex machina
Rusty
Sub

Long ago
Optic lenses
Nighttime
Glow

Ages
Graves
Olden times

Turns out to have been
Oriental influence
Original as fetish (festive)
Kinship expressed vertically

To detect an actual blackhole
Head in the
Early thinkers long ago

Vertical as
Opposed to
Indirection (a turning away from)
Devolved upon

To be artistic and practical
Of the business (world)

Beyond what just was
Earth (en)

Theoretical determination
Harmony of
Ears (eyes)

Passing of years
Reductio ad vertisement
Island
Nope
Childproof
Introductory
Peopled by
Leaps of detection
Emotional involvement (consumption)

Out
Foe

Modernization in all things
Ordnung ordnung
Volunteers
Existence perpetuated by a series of
Marital paradigms
Ends up
Not interested in
Total (remote control)

Negation 9

When in the course of
However unintentional
Accidents do
Turnips tomatoes and taters

Suggestive of
Equilibrium (inner ear)
Eurail (urinal)
Motility (b)
Sonatina

Twigs give
Overly human

Take symmetry
As an instance of
Killing off the least
Ecstasy too has limits

Perfectly aware of
Last but not
Acceptance comes with
Certainty
Elements of logical but

Ovarian cysts might be the cause of
Uterine
Thalassa upon the
Sight of
Inside information
Decadence as a response to
Early millenarian anxiety attacks

In this or that way
The (whole) point of

Topical
Ointment

Breakfast according to
Experts in the nutritional fields

Altogether too much emphasis
Never enough attention to

Acrimony as a symptom of
Criminality
Tested for
Ill ad
Vised
Inves
Tment practices
Yet only if

Dire
Illuminated menus
Rich in
Errata
Cism
Touch restricted to those places
Excavation
Demolition

Alluding to
Grain
As
In the
National interest
Soviet spheres of
Television

If
That had been

If
So facto

If
Then
State meant

Or
Winnowing
Northern climes

Doth toll
Overthrowing
Inverting hierarchical
Not across the
Ground up

Intermittently an at
Tempt to define a hermeneutics of
Sex between consenting pronouns

Orgiastic despair
Wellspring of
Not occurring until

Addressed to
Community of
Three dot breaks
Invaded by
Virtually
Impossible
To
Yet necessary to

Negation 10

Death frames
Entity which differs from itself
A tradition dominated by
There is every reason to
Historically

As
Soon as

Wields
Efface

Mono
Auto
Yet would bespeak

Considerable influence (with)
Angel knows nothing of human fact
Longs for
Lies

Throat
Heart
Arm
Trunk

Unity
Not in origin but destination
Reciprocating verbal assemblage
Exorcism (by means of)
Allotropic
Leanings
Interpretations
Tell the truth
Yell(ow)

In/out
Side

That did not shut out
Homesick
Evil (eventually)

Monological discourse
Ontological insecurity
Syrupy pageant
Testament (to)

The bleeding of colors into the unprimed canvas
Extralexical (read all about it)
Reduced to
Redaction resisting
Intention
But only able to
Limit
Effects of the leftmost

Thanatos
Has taken up
Inside
Nucleic
Genecodings

Anybody
Netted
Debt

Toxic
Overdetermination

Kin ship pivot
Era sure
Ex
Para

Audible
Notes
De(fy)clare

Hankering (after)
Oligarchy
Lilting
Deism

Fabric
Ate
Synopsis
Turnabout is

When vision is the issue
Have at
Autodidact
Tenuous grasp at best

Isometric
Sophistry

Deliberate
Economic projection
Alterity
Defined

Decipherings & disseminations
Earborn
Men(dacities)
Actuarial behavior
Nuptial drearies
Drizzly
Sodden

Truth claims
Herbal (horrible)
Emergency

Green how green
Repeated
Evasion of material circumstance
Apt
Termed yellow is
Examined by a leading
Simplification
Truckstop (tractorpull)

Force (channelled)
Outwit
Reported sightings
Cultured pearls
Each and every

Offal
Flames

After
Last
L

DISPLAYSPACE

for Jake Berry

playing

space

in Alabama

Displayspace 1

with a spirit of attachment   as one attached to   came unglued
buying frenzy   complete liquidation   slashed
each one living with(in) the given   passenger next to me reading *canadian hereford digest*   one more case for the opacity of
tenor   extensive   tension
mose tolliver's impossible creatures   booze or vision   stick to the play ethic
as of yet horses cannot be artificially inseminated   pilot apologizes for having to take several delay vectors   why a sudden respect for the line
in order to graph (wo)man in place among the elements   before this conception becomes obsolete   ponytails of innocence
you are free to move about the cabin   the pride of frankenstein   which is wit which is humor
percolation of the present   so used to her body is he   chuckle of adult men
beaten   portent   tendency

soothing each other by repeating common phrases in expected syntactical patterns
    "so you like american as an airlines"   slap the bourgeoisie & they do strike back
flying within a blinding whiteness the captain consoled himself by studying the green
    glow of his control panel
"you still get four seasons but you don't have to suffer"   "she does a lot of
    contemporary stuff"   "these crystals are *more* beautiful than a work of art"
david holman   bright light   you lying under a tree on a golf course in humid oxford
    mississippi   you dear friend of grace energy & wit outrage & intelligence
    done in by a bad heart at age 38   you are the hole in this poem
"we wouldn't have talked   if we weren't stuck   in this holding pattern"
in the whitney a middle aged woman turned to her companion and said to her "my
    sculpture teacher rents a studio from *elaine* de kooning"
my life had stood a loaded book   helen the hungry bear   helen & the great quiet
michael suggests that new york assigns each activity to a specific locale thus
    sexuality of costume & gesture flourishes on the lower east side
society for the support & training of christian cowboys   the emblem "of"
    emblazoned "upon"
at stake here is not the divination of the secret meaning of the physical world said
    bob pacing back and forth dot dot dot

because loaded down with goods acquired travel back is always more difficult
a shlep   a ship   a shape
chain around her ankle because a sign of
as you're   azure   assure
mumbled interrupted barely social speech habits because no doubt of something way back
swindle   single   swine doll
in the bing & bong because intelligible but barely meaningful
severe   several   sever
because speaker size is not a determining factor
the sire   desire   the sigher

book of ours   greatness & diversity of first quarter of twentieth century begins to
overwhelm us   "as real as it gets"   for to specify is to pacify   the mark of tzara
the return of seltzer   we who loved him knew he had a bad heart but thought that meant
death at 60 not now at 38   couched in   (if not cornered by)   it matters absolutely
[where] on the page   wears on the land   whereupon   or dad's "wherewithall"   hello
dali   young sunk in separate lives   pink flamingo infants where   listen lissen
cop cars revert to black & white   i could do better with more time (/light)   yardbird
parker too young to be inside   servile of the fittest   hair in a bun pulled up into
timeless black religious cap   paint crown molding china white   walls navajo   wind
blow through me   suggestible bells navy blue   in rough trades run a tight ship

cat harriet tubman keeps eating the erasers off my pencils
shout and twist   one dollar perplex   put up prefab autobiography
presidency run as a call-in talkshow   stone commemorates confederate dead
uniforms and barked commands negate humanity   irrecuperable ever irruptive difference
light takes the tree   simple syllables   but who   but how
colonel joe & the bloody corncobs   playing heterogeneous irreducible rocknroll
no hats in class   paging dr. seuss   russo-american utility prejudice
ironically resisting closure over and over   postcard bumpersticker t-shirt paperweight
the pleasure of detest   piss in the mainstream   clean copy
slyly warped   curvature of   coupla couplets   slightly wrapped   tendency toward

lively but stupid

an age of

vertical assertive murder

among serious musicians

looming dwarfed present

verse blown apart

infantilized magician intuits

contends for space

failed in blanks

perched beside forbidden

At lunchtime alone in her office, muttering to herself "simplistic drivel" and "that's absurd," as well she might, reading — the headline BIBLE ENTERS MURDER TRIAL had caught her attention — as she ate a pastrami on rye (promising herself two breath mints after lunch, and sometime, lower cholesterol) she couldn't help but laugh, and why shouldn't she, at the lead paragraph where Mrs. Fowler, the defendant, testified that a day that began with praying and Bible-reading ended in the stabbing death of her husband, and no she could not recall why she selected from eight available knives the boning knife with its sharp point, and why if her husband had tried to choke her the doctor's report made no mention of injuries or bruises, the pastrami sandwich almost finished and her boss bringing by a stack of documents for photocopying and collating.

i awoke and a fever was upon me   led as i was in the first light of morning   early to the writing desk   & there began to put down the words which came to me in rapid & certain order   so steady & intense the fever & the light

"And not only do states have a variable intensity, but different beings 'are' unequally."

blast the exposed twisted cypress roots along this stretch of point lobos coast   where
adams & weston & jeffers each saw gnarled knotted enduring whorls precise signatures
of being & persistence   physical fact   matched exactly to determined seeing

"The sufficiency of each being is endlessly contested by each other."

while admittedly uncertain of the relative worth or excellence of her creation she
nonetheless remained convinced of the uniqueness of her artistic vision   a particular
fusion   (which she left to others to articulate)   of her ministry   christ's grace
blackness   her own poverty   the rural dusty south   her special resistance   to an
increasingly homogenized existence

"Being in fact is found NOWHERE and it was an easy game for a sickly malice to discover it to be divine, at the summit of a pyramid formed by the multitude of beings, which has as its base the immensity of the simplest matter."

though they may have a certain disturbance & resistance in common   suppositions & correspondences which form the base of community   ron's writing differs recognizably & decisively from charles's   and his from lyn's and hers from hannah's and hers from bob's   & any history or criticism of the period   of this style   must also base itself on particularity   on distinction

"*A man is only a particle inserted in unstable and entangled wholes.* ... This extreme instability of connections alone permits one to introduce, as a puerile but convenient illusion, a representation of isolated existence turning in on itself."

she had come to think of herself   particularly as she rode alone from santa rosa to oakland for the 11pm to 11am shift of her nurse's job   as a proposition   biologically speaking   extended   particularized tested out   over space & time   the teasing out   as it were   of the possibilities inherent   in one particular material composition   by virtue of which   she inseparably but not reductively   was

"Abdication and inevitable fatigue — due to the fact that 'being' is, *par excellence*, that which, desired to the point of dread, cannot be endured — plunge human beings into a foggy labyrinth formed by the multitude of 'acquaintances' with which signs of life and phrases can be exchanged."

best western	:	decline of empire
resist utility dances with	:	satisfaction of basic needs
post-democratic	:	post to pill or
bird(blood)bath	:	blurred extinctions
terror	:	eyes firmament
division upon	:	pennants aloft
new suit (yourself)	:	male armor
penance dun	:	perchance to
bring down	:	post up
serve & evade	:	american ends

do & useful   against which root errors   roderick ushered in
an age of discursive poetry   analytic lyric   thought's measure
poesis as conception   [will
                                        you]   text of connective myths
tissues of   fissures in   small lawns   within perfectly   pa-
rameters   by virtue of   over & against   baleful dimension

blurred furnishings of the human being   rented   already fur-
nished   varnished   the very unity of which is in dispute   is
is the crux   since no [divine
                                        beyond] adequates the fractious
when in fact   was never said   the worth of salt   a midday meal
a birth unattended   sun slipping past hazardous angles   figured out later

Displayspace 2

"This curiosity was the way she was, sometimes, with whites.

tea chore   men tore   show me how

Mostly they did not seem quite real to her.

to escape typifying procedures

They seemed very stupid the way they attempted to beat down everybody in their path and then know nothing about it.

indignant ethnographer   fields of synecdoches   these the flowers   this
the anthology   into your hands i place   into the vase   put words in your
mouth   the cadence   sequence of long A's

She saw them sometimes as hordes of elephants, crushing everything underfoot,

the commands "let go" and "gentle"   prove useless

stolid and heavy and yet—unlike the elephant—forgetting."

an ethics of (collage) representation   otherwise known as   other wise

Displayspace 3

idealizing (& using) otherness   in spite of its actually remaining elsewhere

"And indeed, the advent of this anthill society began with the masses,

inward gray steady rainy day   our party departed the next day in search of

who were the first to be subjected to the framework of levelling rationalities.

& numbered among them   narrative patterns   acute observation   accredited with power

The tide rose.

gained purchase

Next it reached the managers who were in charge of the apparatus, managers and technicians absorbed into the system they administered;

commune here we so   (within parentheses lurk unacknowledged subject-positions)

and finally it invaded the liberal professions that thought themselves protected against it, including even men [sic] of letters and artists."

Displayspace 4

when utopia becomes unimaginable when utopia becomes uninhabitable when however
decorated anthill is all that is available
sheer plasticity of the lament as well as subject position determine intensity for
nostalgia and pastoralization of the past vs. purchase power or a suitably
presidential scowl
when one million of their young by occupying a particular place that they might
open it up when the troops disobey & change sides
tender tenement pretender
independent indigenous ethnographers each report a subtle shift hard to
differentiate between resistance and submission
make them talk bring them into the picture wired(tapped) into
who take aimless night walks to orbit outside the tv viewers whose inmost
thoughts (are they)
get not articulated but manifest as conflict & confusion it turns out she did have
residual collision insurance demanding resignation of the older out of touch
precise cost of definition best seen in elective vs. necessary throw it in & mish
it up variations on an old recipe
tent portent existent

hiding out to await his inheritance   crippled will masquerading as restraint and
buddhistic diffidence   waiting for something better to come along
there was every reason in the world not to describe her as she sat writing among books
a radio a computer framed posters and a synthetic mass-produced vaguely asian rug
lacking the knowledge of its own operations   go below vs. go-between   is a medium
is a catalyst is a filament of platinum
the baby sat in the wading pool holding the hosepipe licking slow cold drips laughing
quietly
on the edge of word recognition   when word reached him he had already   of mist and
missed opportunities
talking to the gentle proprietor of the manna grocery health food store she reached
back to pinch and kill the bug crawling across her bare neck
a denominated common person unreflectively telling a personal anecdote   in less than
ten minutes rekeyed the deadbolt   emotion as we've come to know it is scarcely
possible without the introduction of proper names
one holds the line while the other climbs the tree and in every way it is apparent
that one is not exactly like the other
to think tactfully or tactically   she's (he's) all girl (boy)   can he master yet
grasping an object and hitting with it
howard finster servant of god dates & numbers each vision each work of art as in the
angel's golden glitter trumpet & the host of stunned crowding souls flowing out the
hornmouth held by the hand of love: 10:42 P.M., Jan 13, 1988, by Howard Finster
from God, Man of Visions.

because of the diminishing capacity for subjectivity to assert meaningful autonomy
lyric   lark   lurk
and because it conceives of itself as the philosophy of language in practice
lord   lured   lurid
the powerful's favorite narrative exclaims why   because i say so
write   writhe   riot
nuance because new ants tingle your skin
detour   detain   deceive
said because because implies completion (on account of)
set up   set aside   set upon

all the more current "hosepipe" as opposed to plain old "hose" opposable thumb punched up in the air the umpire says you're out bouncier moods than barometric i swear the rubber broke when intercourse of humid events poems made on stolen time once (and again) the poem (is) resisted in the name of the poem tree surgeon vs. groundskeeper vs. yardboy "all along you knew he wasn't really my father but you never told me" pacing back & forth verse turns to vigil these are not the sought after (songs) facts "this lust to be a viewpoint and nothing more" already in transit travelling / theorizing the student-rabbi's stammer focused our attention "mommy cat is making bacon and eggs" in (which) order "what does the dog say" where is the zoo of everyday practices bars bars of my body open we'll take anything everything so strong is our desire to remain alive

with a banjo on my knee   miss sweden   favorite saying
favored to take the title   he always pays for her
in the red   in the square   in the black   i
then friend the circulation of poems became impossible to administer
"no no you say   the pigs say oink   all night
and day"   might the ministers of knowledge acknowledge   but each
speech and every saying varies by circumstance   take it hard
to the hoop   it is an insult to scientific discourse
to make its use merely decorative contrapuntal playful or instantial
three wise men   on the edge of   the na(rra)tivity scene

polka microbial dot

burst urban appendix

unaccountable panoptic administration

into constituent parts

it seems that

warn friends worn

univocal functionalist totalitarianism

resistant brittle play

set in motion

and then again

I feel almost no need to travel for I do not feel especially at home at home. Joe Ackerand David Bibby came highly recommended. On a day about to rain, David pointed to a large house with sprinklers on: "Someone richer than he is smart." Joe grinned & David told the story: "Down in Florida in a crowded parking lot, this old lady in one of them 'Cedes cars was waitin' for a parking space, when up whips this young guy in a sports car, swings in in front of her & steals the space. He gets out of the car & tells the old lady, 'in case you forgot, that's what it feels like to be young.' The lady in the 'Cedes steps on the gas & smashes into the young man's sports car. She gets out, turns to him & says, 'that's what it feels like to be rich & just not give a damn.'" Meanwhile, David holds the line; Joe climbs high from tree to tree sawing off dead branches, lowering the limbs away from the house.

i live in the old snow hinton house of whom david bibby the tree trimmer said there'll
ever be another mayor as good as snow because his yes meant yes his no meant no & if
he showed up a second time at the drinking fountain you knew something was about to happen

"We are subject to, but not identified with, ordinary language. As in the ship of fools, we are embarked, without the possibility of an aerial view or any sort of totalization."

on mondays and thursdays early in the morning he wheeled his baby down the driveway to
watch a huge white garbage truck lift tilt and set down green dumpster after dumpster

"I shall try to describe the erosion that lays bare the ordinary in a body of analytical techniques, to reveal the openings that mark its trace on the borders where a science is mobilized, to indicate the displacements that lead toward the *common place* where 'anyone' is finally silent, except for repeating (but in a different way) banalities."

though forewarned the physician remained inadequately suspicious of an active vaginal
herpes lesion so that labor was too far along for a caesarian to be performed instead
he taped over the sore spot

"a multitude of quantified heroes who lose names and faces as they become the ciphered river of the streets, a mobile language of computations and rationalities that belong to no one."

the head pushes through a dangerous channel

"Like those birds that lay their eggs only in other species' nests, memory produces in a place that does not belong to it."

it fell to the resident   dr. grubbs   to tell the exultant parents of a one in ten
chance that the baby would contract the virus in which case most likely a brain
encephalitis would develop and would if they were lucky kill the child

"In spite of the contrary ideologies that may accompany it, the setting aside of the subject-object relation or of the discourse-object relation is the abstraction that generates an illusion of 'authorship.' It removes the traces of belonging to a network—traces that always compromise the author's rights."

of a piece : of a place

deep dish or thin crust : base or superstructure

can crush an up- : starving in public view

our hope for the future : our hope for the furniture

spell (check) bound : the cystine scalpel

mass transport : business deals and families

will we do : what we will

mineral husbandry : in trace amounts

she was starting : he wouldn't let her leave

down and out : head first

numbered among his close   if the limb in the wind on its own   the cradle will
fall   news (noose) around the world every half hour   newly released
documents   set up a shadow   [take
umbrage]   government   out fitted in the
latest syntactical riggings   dispersed narratives gather in a mosaic display of in-
stitutional force   through tubes and drips force fed the patient   one suspicious

pustule and as a precaution we began antivirals while awaiting results of cultures &
a spinal tap   "& if you become a crocus in a hidden garden   i will become a gardener
& find you"   love of my life   [so runs
my love]   for you   longing all along   al-
most taken from us   our names were numbers anyway   leaving in its place numbness
behind which we hide (play) until a (dismantling) gust comes along   f(th)irst & foremost

Displayspace 5

"And yet his desire to crush all faith in him was in itself built upon

agitation   an urgency akin to sexual   a build up of pressure   as the real
language of men becomes a personal ejaculant squeezed through still
lips & an actual ink pen

a sense of faith. ...There would have to hover above him, like the stars in a full sky,
a vast configuration of images and symbols whose magic and power could lift him up

to fay angels of exacting plagiarists   crowded pinheads of a well-practiced dance
all at a remove from the bacterially sinister pin-prick   the point of which
may well puncture anyone's practical factory

and make him live so intensely that the dread of being black and unequal
would be forgotten; that even death would not matter, that it would be

as with our (suspect rhetorical lipbalm) most extravagant castings about   sightings
& signals beamed back & received   composite retouched image enhancements
prompt curiosity in those primed to be   while cries closer by

a victory. ...But maybe it would never come; maybe there was no such thing for him;
maybe he would have to go to his end just as he was, dumb, driven, with the shadow

of the book depository looming over the ambiguous grassy knoll   ask not for whom the gun
gun barrel stuck in his stomach muffled blast   underfunded federal beneficence
pure products

of emptiness in his eyes. ... 'I hurt folks 'cause I felt I had to; that's all.'"

though then as now calculated upon a return on the investment of our (here meaning
you dear reader & I) reciprocating sympathies   with best wishes from the next life
i had a chance for once and took it to strike back

Displayspace 6

filing under   filling in   or go marching in   or from the margins in   (word)
being as insistence   and in each case

"Their voices were adapted to an imposed context. There was no way to give voice

or song   the cries filtered through reeds   i shall not make beautiful   but
adhere   (seek after which ways i have not yet thought)   stand by   be loyal

to the silences in these histories, to choose the unrecorded. History feeds on

while the shark is attracted to blood   the catfish is a methodical bottom feeder
(and cleans up)

what finds its way into a limited textual record. A historian needs constant

certain recurrent   what the convenience store stocks   (told as companionable
facts)   zip lock bags for the perishables

skepticism and a willingess to read imaginatively, 'against' the sources, to

god   or the thought of such   bright light explodes containing frames
head(land)lock   birth canal   can this be evidence (why him) of a virus

divine what is not represented in the accumulated selection of the archive."

Displayspace 7

start up cost   stardust calls   from birth responsive to voices
acting (up) out   from birth visually exact fixated from the first on bright star
  quilt on the den wall   spatialization & arrangement critical constituents of
  (poesis) textuality
or just one among five or six billion twentieth century births   the memorable not
  found merely or only in sing-song jingle or jump-rope cadence but in conceptuali-
  zation too   as an instance of thought
attention   intention   utensil
[beware panoptical aspirations]   something deadly in cryptology   carping at
  western traditions / white occident ironized vs. something fundamentally
  different
the latter (if climbed up) would alter all   something tells me   double density
free hand   misspell by choice   miss spell by ronco
"why the hell won't she dust when she's told to"   blinds wide open (the drug
  makes) entire network of veins around optic nerve stand exposed   all "quotation"
y'all quotidian   could kiss my way up her thigh   but not in the library
tendollarbill   tengallonhat   tenllgetyouahundred

peel away the dead   blistex is a registered   pre-come fluid
she had taken a big risk in the first place: a major museum mounting a show of the
  typical contents of american women's purses one from each decade of the twentieth
  century
tintop serving pigs feet in the quarters   where are exotic worlds   EVIDENCE OF
  WHAT
he had coined (or quoted—as the two often blur) the phrase "a critical ethnology of
  the quotidian"
he's a man of many chins   a more congenial identification   suitable for
her dreams set most often not where she lives now not this bedroom between her parents
  and the baby but in the house before this one the turquoise house two blocks away
  when there was no baby where her room the converted garage was at the far end of
  the house
forsaking all others   a white science   forsaking all "others"
he knows somewhat that she wants to break up with him to have a less exclusive
  relationship so he for his part refuses to discuss it & calls her a brat
  a bitch & selfish
whole piece sounds like an ending   poet discovers worn out break pads   from
  beginning to
as i felt you slipping away i ran after you crying praying scattering hebrew gutturals
  as charms for my entry into the shadow world and for your return

because of the things that happen out of which nothing (much) can be made
floored   floured   flowered
a vague sense later mulled over because of where things go
diurnal   yearn   durn
plagued by fake theorizing is because
basalt   bassoon   bison
because he must weigh economic opportunity against a commitment to human rights
wet read   dry reed   papyrus
because holding you has always soothed me
dang   fudge   vavoom

into which city (proper name capitalized) rendezvous we   when i thought you were going to die i did not want to go back to see you again   in large part   inland port track lighting   for a gallery effect   spotting   you on a clear plastic tray among the electrodes & monitors   "i don't want payment until you're satisfied"   appetite & stare belie tests which say the disease may have begun   "formerly we had the hegelians, and now the nihilists"   finish what you star   nothing funny about   "only joking" says the rabbit hiding in the bushes chirping like a bird   in the interest of   waiting for what should not be here to appear   does it even make sense to ask who lays claim to a greater realm of truth   mr. bailey & his son david rebuilt the playhouse so that in years to come my son might   better to begin now the process of edging away

"brother   you must scythe your very feet from under you!"
poetry of precision (the authorities) clamp down   story to follow
furthermore   proves to be   un(con)founded   falls close to the tree
Σ (sigma) in his code means a summing up   figment preserves
then redistribute according to earlier plan (which didn't envision these)
subversive pedagogy   dilated pupils   open why   "swing low sweet cadillac"
aggressive upwardly mobile difficult born again disproves blanket version of
tracked down   cracked up   pinned down   pasted up   nude directions
you're the object (alas) of my infections   rose in flames
alabama fred webster carved us a blue-gray choir of angels

virtue oh so

every object modern

perfect sails pitch

affinity vs. coincidence

eurocentric cultural umbrella

her own decision

forge a head

collecting the world

outside the tent

looking for what

Light came in through the sliding glass door. The father was/is a shy man. Mother had to prod dad into giving a book to their son, an illustrated hardbound all about how the human body works book, as prelude to a seemingly overdue conversation about sex. Dad gave him/me the book but dodged for quite a long time the follow up conversation. Until mom made him do it. (Maybe she should have been the one, though that would have been pretty weird.) Shy as he is on this subject, though by all reports he does like to fuck and fairly often, all he could manage was, sitting in his tan rocker in the den, a sidelong glance and a few words: "Got any questions, son, about that book I gave you?" (Genuinely awkward on all accounts, for neither was/is he a bookish man.) To which his eight or nine year old boy said (cocksure?—I don't think so), "Yes. How does the brain work?"

poetry is an answering to that question   is its working (out)   heliotropic with respect
to bright light ([k]not of shipwreck but) of brain   and son   (a *raison* in the son?)

"Everything round him glittered gold and green; in the soft breath of a warm breeze everything stirred gently, all things—the trees, the bushes and the grasses; on every side larks trilled endlessly and ecstatically; the plovers called, weaving in flight over the low-lying meadows or skipping from stump to stump in silence; the rooks strutted about, beautifully and blackly outlined against the tender green background of the as yet short spring corn; darting into rye, which was already slightly tinged with white, they let their heads be seen now and then among its smoky waves."

held torrent held back dammed damned fully effaced whispers of it's too late for so tape it
over blood flesh hair part the head through a dangerous channel emerges into bright light
all about

"His face closely resembled his son's only the forehead was lower and narrower, the mouth a trifle broader, and he seemed always in motion, perpetually shrugging his shoulders as though his suit were too tight for him under the armpits, blinking his eyes, coughing and twitching his fingers, whereas a certain air of detached immobility was his son's distinguishing trait."

i daily began to feel gratitude for my life and for his   and feared this daily feeling   as
the onset of a permanent vulnerability & an imminent mortality   and prayed it wasn't

"'All I wanted to say was that they, my parents, that is, have their minds occupied and do not worry about their own insignificance. It does not stink in their nostrils ....'"

not to take as apparent & as self-evident for the organization of is a constr(i)ucting of & willfulness shall be felt & known as such though pronouns & their offspring take cover

"'As before, I have every wish to lead a useful life, and I still want to devote all my energies to the pursuit of truth; but I can no longer seek my ideal where I did before; I can perceive it now ... much closer to hand.'"

a transfer of allegiance not by treaty & not on some ceremonial plain but fundamental & unchosen visceral as in i would for you my life lay down & no one knows better than to

"'How strange! I want to concentrate and think of death, but I can't even do that. I merely see a patch of sorts ... and that's all.'"

ideologized bodies : bearing scars

baring stars : venom mouse

unreckoned : unrecognized

stick to the subject : socially expected taxidermy

off at my place : strained through a painful

face : nostrils flared

extracranial perception : book(land)speculator

crafty lefty : serves up

frozen rope : dozen roses

hymn big lyric : when describing stop

crossing messages & twisting words helix-wise so that son's & father's words splice in tem
poral procession of con-fused precedence & mixed intent aimed simultaneously at & from for
memory needs objects to be saved [fixing things
between us] in time to be saved out of time
or refuse to sing the too easily true (though half-stammered & clipped is not any the more
honest)   in the name of the son's name for the father   which is not NO   but KNOW

and how   to work (together) even-tempered vigorous ever-determined   though in turning
away a return is predicated upon a single file of well-toned bodies inevitably going over the
edge   *leben und arbeiten*   hard [filling in
the cracks] work hardly working this way caulking
the weathered casings how slow is required in this particular knowing as in imperceptibly
graded dailiness one generation to the next   each furnished with apparent means of embarkation

Displayspace 8

"The return of the subject, however, must be via

writing/reading the range   connections from one to another   factoring in modes of
production & distribution   an exchange between best friends   jazz messengers
trading solos   alternating licks

explicit historical, geographical, political, and social specifications of

a stand in   she had sensed that her career imitated the classification of
flying standby   that is on a space available basis

the location of embodied figures rather than through

to whom is   & who is   read as a function of *from* & *to*   the pure products
of ideology go crazy   selections are made by an anonymous panel of

a reactionary revival of the ideological

who stand in his (commodified mail-order postmodern) shoes (a)

portrait of a timeless humanism."

as hopi prophecy: a container of ashes might one day be thrown from the sky which
could burn the land and boil the oceans   or as our scientists reported to truman:
babies satisfactorily born

Displayspace 9

the grouping of them should be made to seem natural   smile   hold still   that's it

"In the first place, art history tends to see

the one on the left needs to move in a little more   relax your lips   and consider

abstract design, order, and harmony as if they bespoke

not spoken   (speechinterior)   and not that stream of consciousness crap

universal verities that transcend the social formation itself rather than

with no payment in sight and only a slim chance for publication or readership

as manifestations of a society's very desire for

commercials which stand up to a second and third viewing and

the consolation such ideas of order might offer it."

Displayspace 10

when there was to have been   "one of these days"   generated from a passion for
recycling (with a small amount of unusable waste set aside)
landfillsite   waiting to be filled the empty pronouns sat still   continues ex-
panding in your brain (stomach)
assembled from multiples of the ten-second spot   cornered the market (vs. the corner
market)   mom & pop
tenacity   tensile   extend
embarrassed by her father's habit of engaging strangers in conversation   corinna
corinna where can i buy that prismatic commodity charisma   "thank you very much i
appreciate it" (& for emphasis add "you hear")
placed at i level   which is his best   suffer the kant sequences
summer's awinding down   "the president or the drug czar one" (is southern locution
for a binary choice)   the all-time strikeout king
this and so therefore that   f/sound it out   plying the national anathema
"just say dough" (headcold)   is worth an ounce of   extradite dynamite sis boom bah
carton   certain   frighten

the saying goes   & it goes   without saying
one city tears down all billboards in the name of a more attractive business
  climate   while the one i live in puts them up by the dozen in the name of a
  more attractive business climate   each a blind or blinding but not innocent
  moment in capital formation   poetry too based on patterns of figuration dis
  play & removal
friends of the earth   went (or wend) about it   friends of the urge
up observatory hill where edgar poe used to wander during his short stay at the
  university a few tufts of mountain laurel a drab but whispering hillside which
  poe never let appear in his writings but where i had visions & heard voices
  desiring to become the kind of writer i had been reading   the mysticism of
  rilke or maybe lorca   strong calling in an insistent but nondescript setting
headlong or headstrong   light b(l)ends around the   built in conformation to
i toast you & whatever it is you value about yourself i drink to   for i was
  raised in a land where celebration & good feelings were signs of personal
  health if not social gain
each word a room   when one after another they die   and you alone are left
so now when her stomach began to hurt and she lost lots of weight and with it her
  appetite   she let herself drift   ate mostly fried chicken & potato chips   told
  fanya to mind her own business   until doris's confusion—who was who—became all
  there was   and she was lying on her side when the ambulance came and even the
  doctors—fanya's grandson included—had not expected doris to die that night
a polyp grown up from scheduled tasks   more stolen time   i am in poetry
on tonight's phone-in survey we want to know if you think we are still the
  greatestnationonearth   YES votes dial 1-900-444-USA1   NO VOTES DIAL 1-900-USA2
  each phone call costs 50 cents   we want to know what you think

because there's every reason to believe that
when under the sway of   loans & labors   within assimilable dimensions
organic social ensemble because from each a c(h)ording to his knees
sounds about right   (eggs marx the spot)   free floating radical
changed taxonomy because when placed upon the head becomes a hat
say a few words   which pit which peach   fell upon without regard to
all because of the way he hammered home a string of therefores
as these then & when away   like she warned   like she used to say
because on top of that
went bad   want it bad   get away from there

but the soul these days is in different straits   & though our presidents remain a
train of dull & vapid chatterers   we need the assurances airborne   the day of the
soul strutting out on its own & doing a soliloquy is over   thinking marked staccato
hat heart hit hot hurt   i imagine him killing his father smothering him with a pillow
probably only a few days before the old man would have died anyway so resentful had
the son become & so thoroughly had he justified the huge inheritance as rightfully by
now his   tumult   to melt upon vermont   singing repeatedly: "if as a father"   the
rainbow carpet cleaning truck a cover for thieves who clean out the house   life takes
time   complaints & cries fall upon ears attuned to more attractive channels   loss tin
the woods   (in the words)   all else set aside when a certain kind of transmission occurs

a signified masked as   then going in the guise of
returning your gaze (then looking away)   twisting the night away
advertising is my mother tongue   produce basket   upon a hill
overlooking a   exclusive to   guarded by   especially for   exceeding even
as when the celebrated   familiar   known only to a few
she stands one foot turned out   part ballet part over-determination
known so or not   every moment a pose   puffed equipose
tableau me down   invisible until overdone   tenuous command of furniture
embarrassment of ridges   upon the worth of a current activity
acidic fizzle ridges flatten out into a predictably bicameral arrangement

go pounce upon

calibrated to within

frequent liar club

when reminded of

as silly as

she will (won't

she) to work

in the country

of the blond

only fueled speculation

Hours later, my wife offered a suggestion: "It was probably fine, just playing dead. I once had a setter who barked & barked right next to one that wouldn't move." This one lay under the porch. Flies gathered on it. I changed clothes & crawled under to get at it with a shovel. When I bumped it with the shovel, it bared its teeth and hissed. I thought I would bury it as is. Willie, who is sixty and lived for years on a farm near Fayette, said, "my boys would have killed it; put it out of its misery." I did: hit it over the head; dark blood glistened out the mouth. (Silently, I had asked forgiveness before I killed.) Then I buried it. My little boy, Alan, held all the while by Willie, didn't see any of this. I wonder if I did the right thing, now, having no sure way to know whether the possum had indeed been dying or playing.

autonomy drove over me & mowed me down ("shiver me timbers") though levelled came
out ready again to be hopes dashed chained to the (colorized) masthead & instead
became part of a thriving community

"The theory of the self-reproducing universe declares that the Big Bang began as a microscopic quantum fluctuation somewhere in a *previous* universe. Similarly, our own cosmos may be pregnant with other universes—other Big Bang events waiting to happen at any moment—whose explosive births we could only observe with difficulty or perhaps not at all."

yet (& all that "yet" allows) with due allowance for returns in thoreau the sun is
but within localizable domains child of my right hand

"He presented technical arguments for a universe that is an 'eternally existing, self-reproducing entity, that is divided into many mini-universes many of which are much larger than our observable portion. The laws of low-energy physics and even the dimensionality of space-time may be different in each of these mini-universes.'"

is it preferable to teach my son who says "saba" meaning "i can climb in the chair by
myself" that "self" is an outmoded concept that instead he is the intersection of
many forces that he is for the most part determined by them and that very little
is his by him self

"Perhaps even an infinite number of universes could come out from this chaotic field without interfering with one another."

to move something around father son sentence phrase word around the page engaging
eye & ear breath & heart not just for pure interest's sake alone

"Other universes would occasionally be born in, and disappear from, this one with scarcely a whimper. Their 'navel' and our 'umbilical cord,' the pinched tube of space-time joining them at birth, would vanish in a burst of radiation and leave no evidence of maternity."

unfinished by intent   marked by a definite withdrawal   (back into what)

"There is, of course, the semantic question of what distinguishes a natural birth from an artificial one. If intelligent life is seen as the natural consequence of cosmic evolution, then aren't the artifacts of intelligent activity in some sense 'natural'? Intelligent life may be the emergent catalyst for universe creation."

sexes trickery	:	urge to what
quit following me	:	kite flying
lucky lost love	:	second generation bluesman
a woman of	:	implicit sister
left unsaid	:	your right to
whose happy home	:	conventional fixed-rate mortgage
deigned to report	:	dared to repeat
better safe	:	free access
tuned up	:	toned down
spawned its own	:	go out with

we are getting on with it   if   "if as a father"   though rain blurs the ink
| 5750 | anagram & year of miracles   we are going about our   we are minding
our   standing here beyond[to bud &
break off]and before you   becoming more
so all the   crumbling under foot   i who am needy have been afraid of visions
sure it's still the story of the soul's   brown patch spreading is a sure sign of

serious root disease   "vut's the good complaining"   the tension of leaving it just
this way   firm a meant   how can this be that   and when is this that very book you
have been looking for   by[and went
the way]finding it as you write/read (& need) it
left to your own devices   (a)light along the   we are all very busy   righting
it as you go   making a seen   come now   one could have been   one still might be open

Note

Various source materials are used throughout *Three of Ten.* For the curious here is some information about incorporated materials.

H's Journal:

The principle source material is the Journal of Henry David Thoreau. Other books and essays by Thoreau (principally *Walden,* but also some of the last published essays) figure in H's Journal, as do various writings about Thoreau, including Stanley Cavell's *Senses of Walden,* Sharon Cameron's *Writing Nature,* and Richard Lebeaux's two volume biography of Thoreau. Writing by a number of other H's also finds its way into H's Journal — Susan Howe, Lyn Hejinian, and Herman Melville among them — as well as writings by a few irresistible non-H's, especially Emily Dickinson.

Negation:

[This note is reprinted from the paper insert into the audiocassette accompanying the limited edition publication of the book Negation *by Ink-A! Press in 1994.]*
To a certain extent, it began with a reading of certain passages in Hegel's Preface to *Phenomenology of Mind.* I had had certain negations in mind, and reading certain of Hegel's paragraphs gave to those concepts of negation the "positive" content I had been unable until then to find. So phrases from Hegel came to form the vertical top-to-bottom left-hand margin. And these were the phrases I had been dwelling on.

Along the way, two other texts entered in: Lyn Hejinian's *Writing Is An Aid to Memory* and Tom Raworth's *Tottering State* (especially "Ace," "West Wind," and "Tracking [Notes]"). Such, in part, is an affinity of "my line" in *Negation.* And late in the writing of *Negation's* first draft Elizabeth Meese's *Crossing the Double-Cross* entered in.

Pronouns were first in line to get negated. And gradually a determination, in part because of the short phrasal line, to negate the text's (tendency to) running commentary on its own procedures. (Instead, EXPL/NEG.DOC much later?) But of course the tendency toward self-commentary and self-reading is, like the anagrammatic, out of control. Phrases clot into fixed meaning(s) whether I want them to or not.

The vertical phrases laid down via Hegel admit in advance the uncontrollable nature of anagrammatic excess. (The humor being in the complete control exercised in the vertical placement. Therefore, the excess of anagrammatic recombinings beyond my control moves to other sites in the text.)

I went looking for an almost absolute flexibility of phrasal combinings. In many different directions, though primarily along an *x-y* grid (of horizontal and vertical). At times, the possible continuity ends with the single letter. Other times the vertical word marks the boundaries of a continued stanza. And so on. And, at times, there are counter-currents set up — vertical remarks vs. horizontal — while, at other times, the two cooperate with each other. Their relationship is always at issue, and their relationship is always another textual dimension.

Negation is a chapter in a much longer work in progress, *10* x *10*. Along with *H's Journal* and *Displayspace, Negation* constitutes one third of *Three of Ten.*

I was after a means of writing negation which would be an affirmation as well. Contemporarily, such a project would share certain values with the work of Charles Bernstein. And thus too a complex kinship with various forms of irony, not as distancing but in Kierkegaard's conception of it: irony as a withdrawing of content. So that negation, so conceived, becomes a form of inquiry and a method of questioning.

One further negation to bear in mind: the negation of consistent systematization. No one procedure is carried through, no one habit of organization is allowed to become definitive. Thus, the necessity of shifting reading procedures throughout *Negation.*

In short, a negation of certainty through certain operations and procedures. A composition certain from the start to exceed my ability to compose it.

Displayspace:

1 section 8: Georges Bataille, *Visions of Excess*

2 Alice Walker, *Meridian*

3 Michel de Certeau, *The Practice of Everyday Life*

4 section 8: Michel de Certeau, *The Practice of Everyday Life*

5 Richard Wright, *Native Son*

6 James Clifford, *The Predicament of Modern Culture*

7 section 8: Ivan Turgenev, *Fathers and Sons*

8 Gregory Jay, *America the Scrivener*

9 Henry Sayre, *The Object of Performance*

10 section 8: Eugene F. Mallove, "The Self-Reproducing Universe," *Sky and Telescope* 76 (September 1988): 253 – 256

Biographical Note

For over twenty years Hank Lazer has published poetry in many of America's leading journals of experimental writing. His books include *Doublespace: Poems 1971-1989* (Segue), *INTER(IR)RUPTIONS* (Generator Press), *Mouth to Mouth* (Alderman Press), and *Negation* (Ink-A! Press). In addition, two electronic journals, *RIF/T* and *The Experioddicist,* have published chapbooks of Lazer's most recently completed poem series, Days.

In May 1993 Lazer, together with Charles Bernstein and James Sherry, published *Language Poems* (Sichuan Literature & Art Publishing House), a bilingual collection of poems, along with several essays on contemporary American experimental poetry. In conjunction with the publication of this book, Lazer travelled to China to give readings, lectures, and discussions. In 1996 Meow Press published *Early Days of the Lang Dynasty,* a poem written during the China trip.

Lazer has also presented several performance pieces and participated in collaborative performances with other artists, including visual artists and dancers. Lazer is in addition a noted critic of modern and contemporary poetry. His book *Opposing Poetries,* essays on contemporary poetry, was published by Northwestern University Press in 1996. He has also edited two influential books of criticism.

Hank Lazer was born and raised in San Jose, California, received an A.B. degree in English from Stanford University, and holds M.A. and Ph.D. degrees in English from the University of Virginia. A Professor of English at the University of Alabama, where he has taught since 1977, Lazer is currently Assistant Dean for Humanities and Fine Arts.

About the Press

Founded in 1984 in Tucson, Arizona, Chax Press is returning to Tucson as this book is being printed in August 1996, after a 3-year residence in Minneapolis during which the press director, Charles Alexander, served as the Executive Director of Minnesota Center for Book Arts. The press publishes books in editions which explore the possibilities of the art of the book, and in literary trade paperback editions.

Chax Press sponsors events such as literary readings, series of talks by writers and artists, and artists' residencies, in addition to our efforts in book publishing. We are also available for book arts classes, workshops, and lectures, as well as for presentations on contemporary innovative writing.

The typefaces used in *3 of 10* are Adobe Caslon, including Adobe Caslon special fonts and characters. The book has been designed by Charles Alexander. The cover has been designed by Jean Kindem.

Assistance on this book has been provided by Katherine Brown and Cynthia Miller.

Chax Press also thanks William G. Doty, Gregory Jay, and Stan Goodman for their donations which assisted the publication of this book.

Other Chax Press Books

Tom Mandel, *Prospect of Release*
Myung Mi Kim, *The Bounty*
Mary Margaret Sloan, *The Said Lands, Islands, and Premises*
Norman Fischer, *Precisely the Point Being Made*
Nathaniel Tarn, *Caja del Rio*
Rosmarie Waldrop, *Fan Poem for Deshika*
Lisa Cooper, *The Ballad in Memory*

Nathaniel Mackey, *Outlantish*
Ron Silliman, *Demo to Ink*
Beverly Dahlen, *A Reading 8-10*
Gil Ott, *Wheel*
Karen Mac Cormack, *Quirks & Quillets*
Susan Bee & Charles Bernstein, *Fool's Gold*
Sheila Murphy, *Teth*
bp Nichol, *Art Facts: A Book of Contexts*
Charles Bernstein, *Four Poems*
Larry Evers & Felipe S. Molina, *Wo'i Bwikam/Coyote Songs*
Mei-mei Berssenbrugge, *Mizu*
Charles Alexander, *Hopeful Buildings*
Lyn Hejinian & Kit Robinson, *Individuals*
Eli Goldblatt, *Sessions*
John Randolph Hall, *Zootaxy*
Paul Metcalf, *Firebird*
Karl Young, *Five Kwaidan in Sleeve Pages*
Charles Alexander, *Two Songs*
Paul Metcalf, *Golden Delicious*
Jackson Mac Low, *French Sonnets*

Forthcoming in 1996 & 1997 from Chax Press

Karen Mac Cormack, *The Tongue Moves Talk*
Lisa Cooper, *& Calling It Home*
Phillip Foss, *Chromatic Defacement*
Peter Ganick, *Splintered* (part one)